Spurgeon's Sermons on the Sermon on the Mount

by
CHARLES HADDON SPURGEON

Condensed and Edited
By
AL BRYANT

WIPF & STOCK · Eugene, Oregon

Wipf and Stock Publishers
199 W 8th Ave, Suite 3
Eugene, OR 97401

Spurgeon's Sermons on the Mount
Condensed and Edited by Al Bryant
By Spurgeon, Charles H.
ISBN 13: 978-1-5326-1739-3
Publication date 1/27/2017
Previously published by Zondervan, 1956

CONTENTS

CHAPTER ONE

THE BEATITUDES

One enjoys a sermon all the better for knowing something of *the preacher*. It is natural that, like John in Patmos, we should turn to see the voice which spake with us. Turn hither then, and learn that the Christ of God is the Preacher of the Sermon on the Mount. He who delivered the Beatitudes was not only the Prince of preachers, but He was beyond all others qualified to discourse upon the subject which He had chosen. Jesus the Saviour was best able to answer the question, "Who are the saved?" Being Himself the ever-blessed Son of God, and the channel of blessings, He was best able to inform us who are indeed the blessed of the Father. As Judge, it will be His office to divide the blessed from the accursed at the last, and therefore it is most meet that in gospel majesty He should declare the principle of that judgment, that all men may be forewarned.

Do not fall into the mistake of supposing that the opening verses of the Sermon on the Mount set forth how we are to be saved, or you may cause your soul to stumble. You will find the fullest light upon the matter in other parts of our Lord's teaching, but here He discourses upon the question, "Who are the saved?" or, "What are the marks and evidences of a work of grace in the soul?" Who should know the saved so well as the Saviour does? The shepherd best discerns his own sheep, and the Lord Himself alone knoweth infallibly them that are His. We may regard the marks of the blessed ones here given as being

7

the sure witness of truth, for they are given by Him who cannot err, who cannot be deceived, and who, as their Redeemer, knows His own. The Beatitudes derive much of their weight from the wisdom and glory of Him who pronounced them; and, therefore, at the outset your attention is called thereto.

The *occasion* of this sermon is noteworthy; it was delivered when our Lord is described as "seeing the multitudes." He waited until the congregation around Him had reached its largest size, and was most impressed with His miracles, and then He took the tide at its flood, as every wise man should. The sight of a vast concourse of people ought always to move us to pity, for it represents a mass of ignorance, sorrow, sin and necessity, far too great for us to estimate. The Saviour looked upon the people with an omniscient eye, which saw all their sad condition; He saw the multitudes in an emphatic sense, and His soul was stirred within Him at the sight. No one cared for them, they were like sheep without a shepherd, or like shocks of wheat ready to rot for want of harvest-men to gather them in. Jesus therefore hastened to the rescue. Opportunities should be promptly used whenever the Lord puts them in our way. It is good fishing where there are plenty of fish.

The *place* from which these blessings were delivered is next worthy of notice: "Seeing the multitudes, He went up *into a mountain.*" Exalted doctrine might well be symbolized by an ascent to the mount; at any rate, let every minister feel that he should ascend in spirit when he is about to discuss the lofty themes of the Gospel. A doctrine which could not be hid, and which would produce a Church comparable to a city set on a hill, fitly began to be proclaimed from a conspicuous place.

There was instruction in the *posture* of the preacher: "When He was set," He commenced to speak. We do not think that either weariness or the length of the discourse suggested His sitting down. He frequently stood when He preached at considerable length. We incline to the belief that, when He became a pleader with the sons of men, He stood with uplifted hands, eloquent from head to foot, entreating, beseeching and exhorting, with every member of His body, as well as every faculty of His mind; but now that He was, as it were, a Judge awarding the blessings of the kingdom, or a King on his throne, separating His true subjects from aliens and foreigners, He sat down.

It is then added to indicate *the style* of His delivery, that "He opened His mouth." Certain cavillers of shallow wit have said, "How could He teach without opening His mouth?" to which the reply is that He very frequently taught, and taught much, without saying a word, since His whole life was teaching, and His miracles and deeds of love were the lessons of a master instructor. It is not superfluous to say that "He opened His mouth, and taught them," for He had taught them often when His mouth was closed. Jesus Christ spoke like a man in earnest; He enunciated clearly, and spake loudly. He lifted up His voice like a trumpet, and published salvation far and wide, like a man who had something to say which He desired His audience to hear and feel. Oh, that the very manner and voice of those who preach the Gospel were such as to bespeak their zeal for God and their love for souls!

Let us now consider the Beatitudes themselves, trusting that, by the help of God's Spirit, we may perceive their wealth of holy meaning. No words in the compass of Sacred Writ are more precious or more freighted with solemn meaning.

The first word of our Lord's great standard sermon is "Blessed." You have not failed to notice that the last word of the Old Testament is "curse," and it is suggestive that the opening sermon of our Lord's ministry commences with the word "Blessed." Nor did He begin in that manner, and then change His strain immediately, for nine times did that charming word fall from His lips in rapid succession. It has been well said that Christ's teaching might be summed up in two words, "Believe" and "Blessed." Mark tells us that He preached, saying, "Repent ye, and believe the gospel"; and Matthew in this passage informs us that He came saying, "Blessed are the poor in spirit." All His teaching was meant to bless the sons of men; for "God sent not His Son into the world to condemn the world, but that the world through Him might be saved."

The Beatitudes before us, which relate to character, are seven; the eighth is a benediction upon the persons described in the seven Beatitudes when their excellence has provoked the hostility of the wicked; and, therefore, it may be regarded as a confirming and summing up of the seven blessings which precede it. Setting that aside, then, as a summary, we regard the Beatitudes as seven, and will speak of them as such. *The whole seven describe a perfect character, and make up a perfect benediction.*

Observe carefully, and you will see that *each one rises above those which precede it.* The first Beatitude is by no means so elevated as the third, nor the third as the seventh. There is a great advance from the poor in spirit to the pure in heart and the peacemaker. I have said that they rise, but it would be quite as correct to say that *they descend,* for from the human point of view they do so; to mourn is a step below and yet above being poor in spirit, and the peacemaker, while the highest form of Christian, will find himself often called upon to take the lowest room for peace's sake. "The seven Beatitudes mark deepening humiliation and growing exaltation." In proportion as men rise in the reception of the divine blessing, they sink in their own esteem, and count it their honor to do the humblest works.

Not only do the Beatitudes rise one above another, but *they spring out of each other,* as if each one depended upon all that went before. Each growth feeds a higher growth, and the seventh is the product of all the other six. The two blessings which we shall have first to consider have this relation. "Blessed are they that mourn" grows out of "Blessed are the poor in spirit." Why do they mourn? They mourn because they are "poor in spirit." "Blessed are the meek" is a benediction which no man reaches till he has felt his spiritual poverty, and mourned over it. "Blessed are the merciful" follows upon the blessing of the meek, because men do not acquire the forgiving, sympathetic, merciful spirit until they have been made meek by the experience of the first two benedictions. This same rising and outgrowth may be seen in the whole seven.

Mark, also, in this ladder of light, that though each step is above the other, and each step springs out of the other, yet *each one is perfect in itself,* and contains within itself a priceless and complete blessing. The very lowest of the blessed, namely, the poor in spirit, have their peculiar benediction, and indeed it is one of such an order that it is used in the summing up of all the rest. "Their's is the kingdom of heaven" is both the first and the eighth benediction. Highest characters, namely, the peacemakers, who are called the children of God, are not said to be more than blessed; they may enjoy more of the blessedness, but they do not in the covenant provision possess more.

Note, also, with delight, that *the blessing is in every case in the present tense,* a happiness to be now enjoyed and delighted in. It is not "Blessed *shall* be," but "Blessed *are.*" There is not one step in the whole divine experience of the believer, not one link in the wonderful chain of grace, in which there is a withdrawal of the divine smile or an absence of real happiness. Blessed is the first moment of the Christian life on earth, and blessed is the last. Blessed is the spark which trembles in the flax, and blessed is the flame which ascends to heaven in a holy ecstasy. Blessed is the bruised reed, and blessed is that tree of the

Lord, which is full of sap, the cedar of Lebanon, which
the Lord hath planted. Blessed is the babe in grace, and
blessed is the perfect man in Christ Jesus. As the Lord's
mercy endureth for ever, even so shall our blessedness.

We must not fail to notice that, in the seven Beatitudes,
the blessing of each one is appropriate to the character.
"Blessed are the poor in spirit" is appropriately con-
nected with enrichment in the possession of a kingdom
more glorious than all the thrones of earth. It is also most
appropriate that those who mourn should be comforted;
that the meek, who renounce all self-aggrandisement,
should enjoy most of life, and so should inherit the earth.
It is divinely fit that those who hunger and thirst after
righteousness should be filled, and that those who show
mercy to others should obtain it themselves. Who but the
pure in heart should see the infinitely pure and holy God?
And who but the peacemakers should be called the children of the God of peace?

Yet the careful eye perceives that each benediction,
though appropriate, is worded paradoxically. This is
clearly seen in the first Beatitude, for the poor in spirit
are said to possess a kingdom, and is equally vivid in
the collection as a whole, for it treats of happiness, and
yet poverty leads the van, and persecution brings up the
rear; poverty is the contrary of riches, and yet how rich
are those who possess a kingdom! and persecution is supposed to destroy enjoyment, and yet it is here made a subject of rejoicing. See the sacred art of Him who spake as
never man spake. He can at the same time make His words
both simple and paradoxical, and thereby win our attention and instruct our intellects. Such a preacher de-
serves the most thoughtful of hearers.

CHAPTER TWO

THE FIRST BEATITUDE

"Blessed are the poor in spirit: for their's is the kingdom of heaven"—(Matthew 5:3).

Bearing in mind the object of our Saviour's discourse, which was to describe the saved, and not to declare the plan of salvation, we now come to consider the first of the Beatitudes:

"Blessed are the poor in spirit: for their's is the kingdom of heaven."

A ladder, if it is to be of any use, must have its first step near the ground, or feeble climbers will never be able to mount. It would have been a grievous discouragement to struggling faith if the first blessing had been given to the pure in heart; to that excellence the young beginner makes no claim, while to poverty of spirit he can reach without going beyond his line. Had the Saviour said, "Blessed are the rich in grace," He would have spoken a great truth, but very few of us could have derived consolation therefrom. Our Divine Instructor begins at the beginning, with the very ABC of experience, and so enables the babes in grace to learn of Him; had He commenced with higher attainments, He must have left the little ones behind. A gigantic step at the bottom of these sacred stairs would have effectually prevented many from essaying to ascend; but, tempted by the lowly step, which bears the inscription "Blessed are the poor in spirit," thousands are encouraged to attempt the heavenly way.

It is worthy of grateful note that *this gospel blessing
reaches down to the exact spot where the law leaves us
when it has done for us the very best within its power or
design.* The utmost the law can accomplish for our fallen
humanity is to lay bare our spiritual poverty, and convince us of it. It cannot by any possibility enrich a man;
its greatest service is to tear away from him his fancied
wealth of self-righteousness, show him his overwhelming
indebtedness to God, and bow him to the earth in self-
despair. Like Moses, it leads away from Goshen, conducts
into the wilderness, and brings to the verge of an impas-
sable stream, but it can do no more; Joshua Jesus is needed
to divide the Jordan, and conduct into the promised land.
The law rends the goodly Babylonish garment of our
imaginary merits into ten pieces, and proves our wedge
of gold to be mere dross, and thus it leaves us, "naked,
and poor, and miserable." To this point Jesus descends;
His full line of blessing comes up to the verge of destruction, rescues the lost, and enriches the poor. The Gospel
is as full as it is free.

This first Beatitude, though thus placed at a suitably
low point, where it may be reached by those who are in
the earliest stages of grace, is however none the less rich
in blessing. The same word is used in the same sense at
the beginning as at the end of the chain of Beatitudes; the
poor in spirit are as truly and emphatically blessed as the
meek, or the peacemakers. No hint is given as to lower
degree, or inferior measure; but, on the contrary, the very
highest benefit, which is used in the tenth verse as the
gathering up of all the seven Beatitudes, is ascribed to the
first and lowest order of the blessed: "their's is the kingdom of heaven." What more is said even of the co-heirs
with prophets and martyrs? What more indeed could be
said than this? The poor in spirit are lifted from the
dunghill, and set, not among hired servants in the field,
but among princes in the kingdom. Blessed is that soul-

poverty of which the Lord Himself utters such good things. He sets much store by that which the world holds in small esteem, for His judgment is the reverse of the foolish verdict of the proud. As Watson well observes, "How poor are they that think themselves rich! How rich are they that see themselves to be poor! I call it the jewel of poverty. There be some paradoxes in religion which the world cannot understand; for a man to become a fool that he may be wise, to save his life by losing it, and to be made rich by being poor. Yet this poverty is to be striven for more than riches; under these rags is hid, cloth of gold, and out of this carcase cometh honey."

The cause for placing this Beatitude first is found in the fact that *it is first as a matter of experience;* it is essential to the succeeding characters, underlies each one of them, and is the soil in which alone they can be produced. No man ever mourns before God until he is poor in spirit, neither does he become meek toward others till he has humble views of himself; hungering and thirsting after righteousness are not possible to those who have high views of their own excellence, and mercy to those who offend is a grace too difficult for those who are unconscious to their own spiritual need. Poverty in spirit is the porch of the temple of blessedness. As a wise man never thinks of building up the walls of his house till he has first digged out the foundation, so no person skillful in divine things will hope to see any of the higher virtues where poverty of spirit is absent. Till we are emptied of self we cannot be filled with God; stripping must be wrought upon us before we can be clothed with the righteousness which is from heaven.

Christ is never precious till we are poor in spirit, we must see our own wants before we can perceive His wealth; pride blinds the eyes, and sincere humility must open them, or the beauties of Jesus will be for ever hidden from us.

It is worthy of double mention that *this first blessing is given rather to the absence than to the presence of praiseworthy qualities;* it is a blessing, not upon the man who is distinguished for this virtue or remarkable for that excellence, but upon him whose chief characteristic is that he confesses his own sad deficiencies. This is intentional, in order that grace may be all the more manifestly seen to be grace indeed, casting its eye first, not upon purity, but upon poverty; not upon shewers of mercy, but upon needers of mercy; not upon those who are called the children of God, but upon those who cry, "We are not worthy to be called Thy sons." God wants nothing of us except our wants, and these furnish Him with room to display His bounty when He supplies them freely. It is from the worse and not from the better side of fallen man that the Lord wins glory for Himself. Not what I have, but what I have not, is the first point of contact between my soul and God. The good may bring their goodness, but He declares that "there is none righteous, no, not one"; the pious may offer their ceremonies, but he taketh no delight in all their oblations; the wise may present their inventions, but he counts their wisdom to be folly; but when the poor in spirit come to Him with their utter destitution and distress He accepts them at once.

Drawing still nearer to our text, we observe, first, that *the person described has discovered a fact,* he has ascertained his own spiritual poverty; and, secondly, *by a fact he is comforted,* for he possesses "the kingdom of heaven."

1. *The fact which he has ascertained is an old truth,* for the man always was spiritually poor. From his birth he was a pauper, and at his best estate he is only a mendicant. "Naked, and poor, and miserable" is a fair summary of man's condition by nature. He lies covered with sores at the gate of mercy, having nothing of his own but sin, unable to dig and unwilling to beg, and therefore perishing in a penury of the direst kind.

This truth is also universal, for all men are by nature thus poor. In a clan, or a family, there will usually be at least one person of substance, and in the poorest nation there will be some few possessors of wealth; but, alas for our humanity! Its whole store of excellence is spent, and its riches are utterly gone. Among us all, there remains no remnant of good; the oil is spent from the cruse, and the meal is exhausted from the barrel, and a famine is upon us, direr than that which desolated Samaria of old. We owe ten thousand talents, and have nothing wherewith to pay; even so much as a single penny of goodness we cannot find in all the treasures of the nations.

This fact is deeply humiliating. A man may have no money, and yet it may involve no fault, and therefore no shame; but our estate of poverty has this sting in it, that it is moral and spiritual, and sinks us in blame and sin. To be poor in holiness, truth, faith and love of God, is disgraceful to us. Often does the poor man hide his face as one greatly ashamed; far more cause have we to do so who have spent our living riotously, wasted our Father's substance, and brought ourselves to want and dishonor. Descriptions of our state which describe us as miserable are not complete unless they also declare us to be guilty; true, we are objects of pity, but much more of censure. A poor man may be none the less worthy of esteem because of the meanness of his apparel, and the scantiness of his provision; but spiritual poverty means fault, blameworthiness, shame and sin. He who is poor in spirit is therefore a humbled man, and is on the way to be numbered with those that mourn, of whom the second benediction says that "they shall be comforted."

The fact discovered by the blessed one in the text is but little known; the mass of mankind are utterly ignorant upon the matter. Though the truth as to man's lost condition is daily taught in our streets, yet few understand it; they are not anxious to know the meaning of a statement

so uncomfortable, so alarming; and the bulk of those who
are aware of the doctrine, and acknowledge that it is Scrip-
tural, yet do not believe it, but put it out of their thoughts,
and practically ignore it.

*Wherever the truth as to our condition is truly known,
it has been spiritually revealed.* We may say of every one
who knows his soul-poverty, "Blessed art thou, Simon,
son of Jonas, for flesh and blood hath not revealed this
unto thee." To be spiritually poor is the condition of all
men; to be poor in spirit, or to know our spiritual poverty,
is an attainment specially granted to the called and chosen.
An omnipotent hand created us out of nothing, and the
like omnipotence is needed to bring us to feel that we are
nothing. We can never be saved unless we are made alive by
infinite power, nor can we be made alive at all unless that
selfsame power shall first slay us.

It is a sign of grace to know one's need of grace. He
has some light in his soul who knows and feels that he is
in darkness. The Lord Himself has wrought a work of
grace upon the spirit which is poor and needy, and trembles at His Word; and it is such a work that it bears within
it the promise, yea, the assurance of salvation; for the
poor in spirit already possess the kingdom of heaven, and
none have that but those who have eternal life.

One thing is certainly true of the man whose spirit
knows its own poverty, he is in possession of one truth
at least; whereas, before, he breathed the atmosphere of
falsehood, and knew nothing which he ought to know.
However painful the result of poverty of spirit may be,
it is the result of truth; and a foundation of truth being
laid, other truth will be added, and the man will abide
in the truth. All that others think they know concerning
their own spiritual excellence is but a lie, and to be rich
in lies is to be awfully poor. Carnal security, natural
merit, and self-confidence, however much of false peace

they may produce, are only forms of falsehood, deceiving
the soul.

*The position into which a clear knowledge of this one
truth has brought the soul is one peculiarly advantageous
for obtaining every gospel blessing.* Poverty of spirit
empties a man, and so makes him ready to be filled; it
exposes his wounds to the oil and wine of the good
Physician; it lays the guilty sinner at the gate of mercy,
or among those dying ones around the pool of Bethesda
to whom Jesus is wont to come. Such a man opens his
mouth, and the Lord fills it; he hungers, and the Lord
satisfies him with good things. Above all other evils we
have most cause to dread our own fulness; the greatest
unfitness for Christ is our own imaginary fitness. When
we are utterly undone, we are near to being enriched with
the riches of grace. Out of ourselves is next door to being
in Christ. Where we end, mercy begins; or rather, mercy
has begun, and mercy has already done much for us when
we are at the end of our merit, our power, our wisdom,
and our hope.

A man may be so misled, however, as to make a merit
out of his sense of sin, and may dream of coming to Jesus
clothed in a fitness of despair and unbelief; this is, however, the very reverse of the conduct of one who is poor
in spirit, for he is poor in feelings as well as in everything
else, and dares no more commend himself on account of
his humblings and despairings than on account of his sins
themselves. He thinks himself to be a hardhearted sinner as he acknowledges the deep repentance which his
offences call for; he fears that he is a stranger to that
sacred quickening which makes the conscience tender, and
he dreads lest he should in any measure be a hypocrite in
the desires which he perceives to be in his soul.

It may seem to some to be a small matter to be poor
in spirit; let such persons remember that *our Lord so
places this gracious condition of heart that it is the foun-*

dation-stone of the celestial ascent of Beatitudes; and who can deny that the steps which rise from it are beyond measure sublime? It is something inexpressibly desirable to be poor in spirit if this be the road to purity of heart, and to the godlike character of the peacemaker.

II. Having spoken thus much upon the character of those who are poor in spirit as being formed by the knowledge of a fact, we have now to note that *it is by a fact that they are cheered and rendered blessed*: "for their's is the kingdom of heaven."

It is not a promise as to the future, but a declaration as to the present; not their's *shall* be, but "their's *is* the kingdom of heaven." This truth is clearly revealed in many Scriptures by necessary inference; for, first, *the King of the heavenly kingdom is constantly represented as reigning over the poor.* David says, in the seventy-second Psalm, "He shall judge the poor of the people, He shall save the children of the needy. . . . He shall spare the poor and needy, and shall save the souls of the needy." As His virgin mother sang, "He hath put down the mighty from their seats, and exalted them of low degree. He hath filled the hungry with good things; and the rich He hath sent empty away." Those who enlist beneath the banner of the Son of David are like those who of old came to the son of Jesse in the cave of Adullam, "Every one that was in distress, and every one that was in debt, and every one that was discontented, gathered themselves unto him; and he became a captain over them." "This Man receiveth sinners and eateth with them." His title was "a Friend of publicans and sinners." "Though He was rich, yet for our sakes He became poor," and it is therefore meet that the poor should be gathered unto Him. Since Jesus has chosen the poor in spirit to be His subjects, and said, "Fear not, little flock; for it is your Father's good pleasure to give you the kingdom," we see how true it is that they are blessed.

*The rule of the kingdom is such as only the poor in
spirit will endure.* To them it is an easy yoke from which
they have no wish to be released; to give God all the
glory is no burden to them, to cease from self is no hard
command. The place of lowliness suits them, the service of
humiliation they count an honor; they can say with the
psalmist (Ps. 131:2), "Surely I have behaved and quieted
myself, as a child that is weaned of his mother: my soul is
even as a weaned child." Self-denial and humility, which
are main duties of Christ's kingdom, are easy only to
those who are poor in spirit. A humble mind loves humble
duties, and is willing to kiss the least flower which grows
in the Valley of Humiliation; but to others a fair show in
the flesh is a great attraction, and self-exaltation the main
object of life; Our Saviour's declaration "Except ye be
converted, and become as little children, ye shall not enter
into the kingdom of heaven," is an iron rule which shuts
out all but the poor in spirit; but, at the same time, it is
a gate of pearl which admits all who are of that character.

*The privileges of the kingdom are such as only the spirit-
ually poor will value;* to others, they are as pearls cast
before swine. The self-righteous care nothing for pardon,
though it cost the Redeemer His life's blood; they have no
care for regeneration, though it be the greatest work of
the Holy Spirit; and they set no store by sanctification,
though it is the Father Himself who has made us meet to
be partakers of the inheritance of the saints in light. Evidently the blessings of the covenant were meant for the
poor in spirit; there is not one of them which would be
valued by the Pharisee. A robe of righteousness implies
our nakedness; manna from heaven implies the lack of
earthly bread. Salvation is vanity if men are in no danger,
and mercy a mockery if they be not sinful.

Moreover, *it is clear that only those who are poor in
spirit do actually reign as kings unto God.* The crown of

this kingdom will not fit every head; in fact, it fits the
brow of none but the poor in spirit. No proud man reigns;
he is the slave of his boastings, the serf of his own lofti-
ness. The ambitious worldling grasps after a kingdom,
but he does not possess one; the humble in heart are content, and in that contentment they are made to reign.
High spirits have no rest; only the lowly heart has peace.
To know one's self is the way to self-conquest, and self-
conquest is the grandest of all victories. The world looks
out for a lofty, ambitious, stern, self-sufficient man, and
says he bears himself like a king: and yet, in very truth,
the real kings among their fellows are meek and lowly
like the Lord of all, and in their unconsciousness of self
lies the secret of their power. The kings among mankind
the happiest, the most powerful, the most honorable, will
one day be seen to be, not the Alexanders, Caesars and
Napoleons, but the men akin to Him who washed the
disciples' feet, those who in quietness lived for God and
their fellow-men, unostentatious because conscious of their
failures, unselfish because self was held in low esteem,
humble and devout because their own spiritual poverty
drove them out of themselves, and led them to rest along
upon the Lord.

*The dominion awarded by this Beatitude to the poor in
spirit is no common one;* it is the kingdom of heaven, a
heavenly dominion, far excelling anything which can be
obtained this side of the stars. An ungodly world may
reckon the poor in spirit to be contemptible but God
writes them down among His peers and princes; and His
judgment is true, and far more to be esteemed than the
opinions of men or even of angels.

"Poor in spirit"; the words sound as if they described
the owners of nothing, and yet they describe the inheritors
of all things. Happy poverty! Millionaires sink into insig-
nificance, the treasures of the Indies evaporate in smoke,
while to the poor in spirit remains a boundless, endless,

faultless kingdom, which renders them blessed in the esteem of Him who is God over all, blessed for ever. And all this is for the present life in which they mourn, and need to be comforted, hunger and thirst, and need to be filled; all this is for them while yet they are persecuted for righteousness' sake; what then must be their blessedness when they shall shine forth as the sun in the kingdom of their Father, and in them shall be fulfilled the promise of their Master and Lord, "to him that overcometh will I grant to sit with Me in My throne, even as I also over came, and am set down with My Father in His throne."

CHAPTER THREE

THE THIRD BEATITUDE

"Blessed are the meek: for they shall inherit the earth"—(Matthew 5:5).

I have often reminded you that the beatitudes rise one above the other, and spring out of one another, and that those which come before are always necessary to those that follow after. This third beatitude, "Blessed are the meek," could not have stood first—it would have been quite out of place there. When a man is converted, the first operation of the grace of God within his soul is to give him true poverty of spirit, so the first beatitude is, "Blessed are the poor in spirit." The Lord first makes us know our emptiness and so humbles us; and then, next, He makes us mourn over the deficiencies that are so manifest in us. Then comes the second beatitude: "Blessed are they that mourn." First there is a true knowledge of ourselves; and then a sacred grief arising out of that knowledge. Now, no man ever becomes truly meek, in the Christian sense of that word, until he first knows himself, and then begins to mourn and lament that he is so far short of what he ought to be. Self-righteousness is never meek; the man who is proud of himself will be quite sure to be hard-hearted in his dealings with others. To reach this rung of the ladder of light, he must first set his feet upon the other two. There must be poverty of spirit and mourning of heart before there will come that gracious meekness of which our text speaks.

24

Note too, that this third beatitude is of a higher order than the other two. There is something positive in it, as to virtue. The first two are rather expressive of deficiency, but here there is a something supplied. A man is poor in spirit; that is, he feels that he lacks a thousand things that he ought to possess. The man mourns; that is, he laments over his state of spiritual poverty. But now there is something really given to him by the grace of God—not a negative quality, but a positive proof of the work of the Holy Spirit within his soul, so that he has become meek. The first two characters that receive a benediction appear to be wrapped up in themselves. The man is poor in spirit; that relates to himself. His mourning is his own personal mourning which ends when he is comforted; but the meekness has to do with other people. It is true that it has a relationship to God, but a man's meekness is especially toward his fellowmen. He is not simply meek within himself; his meekness is manifest in his dealings with others. You would not speak of a hermit, who never saw a fellow-creature, as being meek; the only way in which you could prove whether he was meek would be to put him with those who would try his temper. So that this meekness is a virtue, larger, more expansive, working in a wider sphere than the first two characteristics which Christ has pronounced blessed. It is superior to the others, as it should be, since it grows out of them; yet, at the same time, as there is, through the whole of the beatitudes, a fall parallel with the rise, so is it here. In the first case, the man was poor, that was low; in the second case, the man was mourning, that also was low; but if he kept his mourning to himself, he might still seem great among his fellow-men. But now he has come to be meek among them —lowly and humble in the midst of society, so that he is going lower and lower; yet he is rising with spiritual exaltation, although he is sinking as to personal humiliation, and so has become more truly gracious.

Now, having spoken of the connection of this beatitude, we will make two inquiries with the view of opening it up. They are these—first, *who are the meek?* and, secondly, *how and in what sense can they be said to inherit the earth?*

I. First, then, *who are the meek?*

I have already said that they are those who have been made poor in spirit by God, and who have been made to mourn before God, and have been comforted; but here we learn that they are also meek, that is, lowly and gentle in mind before God and before men.

They are meek before God, and good old Watson divides that quality under two heads, namely, that they are submissive to His will, and flexible to His Word. May these two very expressive qualities be found in each one of us!

So the truly meek are, first of all, *submissive to God's will.* Whatever God wills, they will. With such a happy, contented spirit as that, those who are meek do not quarrel with God. They do not talk, as some foolish people do, of having been born under a wrong planet, and placed in circumstances unfavorable to their development. And even when they are smitten by God's rod, they do not rebel against Him, and call Him a hard Master; but they are either dumb with silence, and open not their mouth because God hath done it, or if they do speak, it is to ask for grace that the trial they are enduring may be sanctified to them, or they may even rise so high in grace as to glory in infirmities, that the power of Christ may rest upon them. The proud-hearted may, if they will, arraign their Maker, and the thing formed may say to Him who formed it, "Why hast Thou made me thus?" But these men of grace will not do so. It is enough for them if God wills anything; if He wills it, so let it be—Solomon's throne or Job's dung-hill; they desire to be equally happy wherever the Lord may place them, or however He may deal with them.

They are also *flexible to God's Word;* if they are really meek, they are always willing to bend. They do not imagine what the truth ought to be, and then come to the Bible for texts to prove what they think should be there; but they go to the inspired Book with a candid mind, and they pray, with the psalmist, "Open Thou mine eyes, that I may behold wondrous things out of Thy law." And when, in searching the Scriptures, they find deep mysteries which they cannot comprehend, they believe where they cannot understand; and where, sometimes, different parts of Scripture seem to conflict with one another, they leave the explanation to the great Interpreter who alone can make all plain. When they meet with doctrines that are contrary to their own notions, and hard for flesh and blood to receive, they yield up themselves to the Divine Spirit, and pray, "What we know not, teach Thou to us." When the meek in spirit find, in the Word of God, any precept, they seek to obey it at once. The meek in spirit are like a photographer's sensitive plates, and as the Word of God passes before them, they desire to have its image imprinted upon their hearts. Their hearts are the fleshly tablets on which the mind of God is recorded; God is the Writer, and they become living epistles, written, not with ink, but with the finger of the living God. Thus are they meek toward God.

But meekness is a quality which also relates largely to men; and I think it means, first, that *the man is humble.* He bears himself, among his fellow-men, not as a Caesar who, as Shakespeare says, doth "bestride the narrow world like a Colossus," beneath whose huge legs ordinary men may walk, and peep about to find themselves dishonorable graves; but he knows that he is only a man, and that the best of men are but men at the best, and he does not even claim to be one of the best of men. He knows himself to be less than the least of all saints; and, in some respects, the very chief of sinners. The meek-spirited man is always of a humble temper and carriage. He is the very opposite of the proud man. Humility, although it is not all that there is in meekness, is one of the chief characteristics of it.

Out of this grows gentleness of spirit. *The man is gentle;* he does not speak harshly; his tones are not imperious, his spirit is not domineering. He will often give up what he thinks to be lawful, because he does not think it is expedient for the good of others. He seeks to be a true brother among his brethren, thinks himself most honored when he can be the doorkeeper of the house of the Lord, or perform any menial service for the household of faith.

In addition to being humble and gentle, *the meek are patient.* They know "it must needs be that offences come"; yet they are too meek either to give offence or to take offence. If others grieve them, they put up with it. They do not merely forgive seven times, but seventy times seven; in fact, they often do not feel as if anything had been done that needed any forgiveness, for they have not taken it as an affront.

But since this is a wicked world, and there are some men who will persecute us, and others who will try to rob us of our rights, and do us serious injury, the meek man goes beyond merely bearing what has to be borne, for *he freely forgives the injury that is done to him.* It is an ill sign when any one refuses to forgive another. Do you know that God will never hear your prayer for forgiveness until you forgive others? That is the very condition which Christ taught His disciples to present: "Forgive us our debts, as we forgive our debtors." If thou takest thy brother by the throat, because he oweth thee a hundred pence, canst thou think that God will forgive thee the thousand talents which thou owest to Him? So the meek-spirited man forgives those who wrong him; he reckons that injuries are permitted to be done to him as trials of his grace, to see whether he can forgive them, and he does so, and does so right heartily.

I think that meekness also involves *contentment*. The meek-spirited man is not ambitious; he is satisfied with what God provides for him. He does not say that his soul loathes the daily manna, and the water from the rock never loses its sweetness to his taste. His motto is. "God's providence is my inheritance." He has his ups and his downs, but he blesses the Lord that his God is a God of the hills, and also of the valleys; and if he can have God's face shining upon him, he cares little whether it be hills or valleys upon which he walks. He is content with what he has, and he says, "Enough is as good as a feast." Whatever happens to him, seeing that his times are in God's hand, it is well with him, in the best and most emphatic sense.

Put those five qualities together, and you have the truly meek man—humble, gentle, patient, forgiving and contented; the very opposite of the man who is proud, harsh, angry, revengeful and ambitious. It is only the grace of God, as it works in us by the Holy Spirit, that can make us thus meek.

II. Now, in the second place, let us think of *how the meek inherit the earth.*

Jesus said, "Blessed are the meek: for they shall inherit the earth." This promise is similar to the inspired declaration of Paul, "Godliness is profitable unto all things, having promise of the life that now is, and of that which is to come." So, first, it is the meek man who inherits the earth, for *he is the earth's conqueror.* He is the conqueror of the world wherever he goes. The Christian conqueror wins his victories by the weapons of kindness and meekness. In the Puritan times, there was an eminent and godly minister, named Mr. Deering, who has left some writings that are still valuable. While sitting at a table one day, a graceless fellow insulted him by throwing a glass of beer in his face. The good man simply took his handkerchief, wiped his face, and went on eating his dinner. The man provoked him a second time by doing the same thing, and he even did it a third time with many oaths and blasphemy. Mr. Deering made no reply, but simply wiped his face; and on the third occasion, the man came, and fell at his feet, and said that the spectacle of his Christian meekness, and the look of tender, pitying love that Mr. Deering had cast upon him, had quite subdued him. So the good man was the conqueror of the bad one. No Alexander was ever greater than the man who could bear such insults like that.

The meek inherit the earth in another sense, namely, that *they enjoy what they have.* If you find me a man who thoroughly enjoys life, I will tell you at once that he is a meek, quiet-spirited man. Enjoyment of life does not consist in the possession of riches. There are many rich men who are utterly miserable, and there are many poor men who are equally miserable. You may have misery, or you may have happiness, according to your state of heart in any condition of life. The meek man is thankful, happy and contented, and it is contentment that makes life enjoyable.

"Oh!" says someone, "But that is not inheriting the earth; it is only inheriting a part of it." Well, it is inheriting as much of it as we need, and there is a sense in which the meek do really inherit the whole earth. I have often felt, when I have been in a meek and quiet spirit, as if everything around belonged to me. I have walked through a gentleman's park, and I have been much obliged to him for keeping it in such order on purpose for me to walk through it. I have gone inside his house, and seen his picture gallery, and I have been grateful to him for buying such grand pictures, and I have hoped that he would buy a few more so that I might see them when I

came next time. I was glad that I had not to buy them,
and to pay the servants to watch over them, and that
everything was done for me. And I have sometimes
looked from a hill, upon some far-reaching plain,
or some quiet village, or some manufacturing town,
crowded with houses and shops, and I have felt that they
were all mine, although I had not the trouble of collect-
ing the rents which people perhaps might not like to pay.
I had only to look upon it all as the sun shone upon it,
and then to look up to heaven, and say, "My Father, this
is all Thine; and, therefore, it is all mine; for I am an heir
of God, and a joint-heir with Jesus Christ." So, in this
sense, the meek-spirited man inherits the whole earth.

Again, the meek-spirited man inherits the earth in this
sense—*if there is anyone who is good anywhere near him,
he is sure to see him.* I have known persons to join the
church, and after they have been a little while in it, they
have said, "There is no love there." Now, when a brother
says, "There is no love there," I know that he has been
looking in the glass, and that his own reflection has suggested his remark. Such persons cry out about the decep-
tions and hypocrisies in the professing church, and they
have some cause for doing so; only it is a pity that they
cannot also see the good people, the true saints, who are
there. The Lord still has a people who love and fear
Him, a people who will be His in the day when He makes
up His jewels; and it is a pity if we are not able to see
what God so much admires. If we are meek, we shall
the more readily see the excellences of other people.
There is a beautiful passage, in the second part of *The
Pilgrim's Progress,* which tells that, when Christiana and
Mercy had both been bathed in the bath, and clothed in
the fine linen, white and clean, "they began to esteem each
other better than themselves." If we also do this, we shall
not think so badly as some of us now do of this poor

present life, but shall go through it thanking God, and praising His name, and so inheriting the earth.

With a gentle temper, and a quiet spirit, and grace to keep you so, you will be inheriting the earth under any circumstances. If trouble should come, you will bow to it, as the willow bows to the wind, and so escapes the injury that falls upon sturdier trees. If there should come little vexations, you will not allow yourself to be vexed by them; but will say, "With a little patience, they will all pass away."

But the text means more than I have yet said, for the promise, "they shall inherit *the earth*," may be read, "they shall inherit *the land*," that is, the promised land, the heavenly Canaan. These are the men who shall inherit heaven, for up there they are all meek-spirited. There are no contentions there; pride cannot enter there. Anger, wrath, and malice never pollute the atmosphere of the celestial city. There, all bow before the King of kings, and all rejoice in communion with Him and with one another. Ah, beloved, if we are ever to enter heaven, we must fling away ambition, and discontent, and wrath, and self-seeking, and selfishness. May God's grace purge us of all these; for, as long as any of that evil leaven is in our soul, where God is we cannot go.

And then the text means yet more than that—we shall inherit this earth by-and-by. David wrote, "The meek shall inherit the earth; and shall delight themselves in the abundance of peace." After this earth has been purified by fire, after God shall have burned the works of men to ashes, and every trace of corrupt humanity shall have been destroyed by the fervent heat, then shall this earth be fitted up again, and angels shall descend with new songs to sing, and the New Jerusalem shall come down out of heaven from God in all her glory. And then upon this earth, where once was war, the clarion shall ring no more; there shall be neither swords nor spears, and men shall learn the arts of war no more. The meek shall then possess the land, and every hill and valley shall be glad, and every fruitful plain shall ring with shoutings of joy, and peace, and gladness.

But this must be the work of grace. We must be born again, or else our proud spirits will never be meek. And if we have been born again, let it be our joy, as long as we live, to show that we are the followers of the meek and lowly Jesus, with whose gracious words I close my discourse, "Come unto Me, all ye that labour and are heavy laden, and I will give you rest. Take my yoke upon you, and learn of Me; for I am meek and lowly in heart, and ye shall find rest unto your souls. For My yoke is easy, and My burden is light." So may it be, for Christ's sake! Amen.

Chapter Four

THE HUNGER AND THIRST WHICH ARE BLESSED

> *"Blessed are they which do hunger and thirst after righteousness: for they shall be filled"*—(Matthew 5:6).

Because man had perfect righteousness before the fall, he enjoyed perfect blessedness. If you and I shall, by divine grace, attain to blessedness hereafter, it will be because God has restored us to righteousness. As it was in the first paradise, so must it be in the second—righteousness is essential to the blessedness of man. We cannot be truly happy and live in sin. Holiness in the natural element of blessedness; and it can no more live out of that element than a fish could live in the fire. The happiness of man must come through his righteousness: his being right with God, with man, with himself—indeed, his being right all round. Since, then, the first blessedness of our unfallen state is gone, and the blessedness of perfection hereafter is not yet come, how can we be blessed in the interval which lies between? The answer is, "Blessed are they which do hunger and thirst after righteousness." Though they have not yet attained the righteousness they desire, yet even the longing for it makes them a blessed people. The massive blessedness of the past, and the priceless blessedness of the eternal future, are joined together by a band of present blessedness. The band is not so massive as those two things which it unites; but it is of the same metal, has been fashioned by the same hand, and is

34

as indestructible as the treasures which it binds together.

First, then, in our text we have mention of *singular appetites*—"hunger and thirst," not for bread and water, but, "after righteousness"; secondly, we have a *remarkable declaration* about these hungering people—Jesus says that they are "blessed," or happy; and beyond a doubt His judgment is true. Thirdly, in our text is mentioned a *special satisfaction* meeting their necessity, and in its foresight making them blessed: our Saviour says, "they shall be filled."

I. To begin, then, we shall speak of *singular appetites.*

In this case, *one insatiable desire takes different forms.* They hunger and they thirst: the two most urgent needs of the body are used to set forth the cravings of the soul for righteousness. Hunger and thirst are different, but they are both the language of keen desire. He that has ever felt either of these two knows how sharp are the pangs they bring; and if the two are combined in one craving, they make up a restless, terrible, unconquerable passion. Who shall resist a man hungering and thirsting? His whole being fights to satisfy his awful needs. Blessed are they that have a longing for righteousness, which no one word can fully describe, and no one craving can set forth. Hunger must be joined with thirst, to set forth the strength and eagerness of the desire after righteousness.

These appetites are concentrated upon one object: the man hungers and thirsts after righteousness, and nothing else. Theological works mostly say either that this is imputed righteousness, or implanted righteousness. No doubt these things are meant, but I do not care to insert an adjective where there is none. It is righteousness which the man pants after: righteousness in all its meanings. First, he feels that he is not right with God, and the discovery causes him great distress. The Spirit of God shows him that he is all wrong with God, for he has broken the law which he ought to have kept, and he has not paid the

homage and love which were justly due. The same Spirit
makes him long to get right with God; and, his conscience
being aroused, he cannot rest till this is done. This, of
course, includes the pardon of his offenses, and the giving
to him of a righteousness which will make him acceptable
to God: he eagerly cries to God for this boon. One of the
bitterest pangs of his soul-hunger is the dread that this
need can never be met. How can man be just with God?
It is the peculiar glory of the Gospel that it reveals the
righteousness of God—the method by which sinners can
be put right with God; and this comes with peculiar sweetness to one who is striving and praying, hungering and
thirsting after righteousness. When he hears of righteousness by faith in the Lord Jesus Christ, he leaps at it, and
lays hold upon it, for it exactly meets his case.

The hunger now takes another form. The pardoned and
justified man now desires to be right in his conduct, and
language, and thought: he pines to be righteous in his
whole life. He would be marked by integrity, kindness,
mercifulness, love and everything else which goes to make
up a right condition of things toward his fellow-creatures.
He ardently desires to be correct in his feelings and conduct toward God: he craves rightly to know, obey, pray,
praise and love his God. He cannot rest till he stands
toward God and man as he ought to stand.

But, mark you, if the man should even attain to this,
his hunger and thirst would only take another direction.
The godly man hungers and thirsts to see righteousness
in others. At times, when he sees the conduct of those
around him, he cries, "My soul is among lions; and I lie
even among them that are set on fire." The more holy he
becomes, the more sin vexes his righteous soul.

Note well that these *concentrated appetites are very
discriminating.* The man does not long for twenty things,
but only for one thing, and for that one thing by itself.
The hunger and the thirst are "after righteousness." The

man does not hunger for wealth: he would rather be poor
and be righteous, than be rich through evil. He does not
hunger after health, though he would wish to have that
great blessing, yet he would rather be sick and have righteousness, than enjoy good health and be unrighteous. He
does not even set before himself, as his great object, the
rewards of righteousness. These are desirable: the respect
of one's fellows, peace of mind, and communion with God,
are by no means little things; but he does not make these
the chief objects of his desire, for he knows that they will
be added to him if in the first place he seeks after righteousness itself. If there were no heaven, the godly man
would wish to be righteous; if there were no hell, he
would dread unrighteousness. His hunger and thirst are
after honesty, purity, rectitude and holiness: he hungers
and he thirsts to be what God would have him to be.

Many refuse the Lord Jesus Christ, who is the Bread
of heaven. No man can be said to be hungry if he refuses
wholesome food. When your child sits down to table, and
says that he does not want any dinner, he is evidently not
hungry. They who put Christ away, and will not have
His atonement, and His sanctification, are not hungry after
righteousness. Many criticize the little things of the Gospel,
the insignificant matters about the minister's voice, and
tone, and appearance. When a man sits down to dinner,
and begins to notice that one of the dishes is chipped, and
one of the roses in the center has an insect on it, and the
salt-cellar is not in the right position to half an inch, and
the parsley is not nicely arranged around the cold meat,
that fellow is not hungry.

II. I have feebly given you the description of the character, and now I come to notice the *remarkable declaration*
of our Lord. He says, "Blessed are they which do hunger
and thirst after righteousness."

Why are you blessed? Well, first, because *Jesus says
you are;* and if He says it, we do not need any further

proof. If, looking around on the crowd, our Lord passes
by those who are self-satisfied; and if His eyes light on
the men that sigh, and cry, and hunger, and thirst after
righteousness, and if, with smiling face, He says, "These
are the blessed ones," then depend upon it, they are so;
for I wot that those whom He declares to be blessed must
be blessed indeed. I would rather be one whom Christ
counted blessed than one who was so esteemed by all the
world, for the Lord Jesus knows better than men do.

The man hungering after righteousness ought to consider
himself a happy man, because *he has been made to know
the right value of things*. Before, he set a high value upon
worthless pleasure, and he reckoned the dross of the praise
of men to be as pure gold; but now, he values righteousness, and is not as the child who prizes glass beads more
than pearls. He has already obtained some measure of
righteousness, for his judgment reckons rightly.

Observe, further, that not only does he estimate things
correctly, but *he has a heart toward that which is good
and desirable*. Once he only cared for earthly comforts;
now he hungers and thirsts after righteousness. "Give me
a bit of meat in the pot," cries the worldling, "and I will
leave your precious righteousness to those who want it";
but this man prizes the spiritual above the natural, righteousness is happiness to him.

He is blessed because, in the presence of this hunger,
many meaner hungers die out. One master-passion, like
Aaron's rod, swallows up all the rest. He hungers and
thirsts after righteousness; and, therefore, he has done
with the craving of lust, the greed of avarice, the passion
of hate, the pining of ambition. We have known sickly
men to be overtaken by a disease which has driven out
their old complaints, a fresh fire has put out the former
ones. So men, under the influence of a craving for righteousness, have found land-hunger, and gold-hunger, and

pride-thirst, and lust-thirst come to an end. The new affections have expelled the old.

These men are blessed by being *delivered from many
foolish delusions.* The delusion is most common, that man
can get everything that he needs in religion out of himself. Most men are deluded in this way—they think they
have a springing well of power within, from which they
can cleanse, and revive, and satisfy themselves. They
imagine that they can, by an effort of their own, satisfy
conscience, make themselves pure, and produce righteousness of character. Still do they dream of bringing a clean
thing out of an unclean.

Once again, these men are blessed because *they are
already worked upon by the Holy Ghost.* Hunger and
thirst after righteousness are always the production of
the Holy Spirit. It is not natural to man to love the good
and the holy; he loves that which is wrong and evil; he
loves the trespass or the omission, but strict rectitude
before God he does not seek after. But when a man is hungry to be true, hungry to be sober, hungry to be pure, hungry to be holy—his hunger is a boon from heaven, and a
pledge of the heaven from which it came.

Once more: this man is blessed, for *in his hunger and
thirst he is in accord with the Lord Jesus Christ.* When
our Lord was here, He hungered after righteousness, longing to do and suffer His Father's will. His disciples, on
one occasion, went away to the city to buy meat; and He,
being left alone, thirsted to bless the poor sinful woman
of Samaria, who came to the well to draw water. To
her He said, "Give me to drink," not only to commence
the conversation, but because He thirsted to make that
woman righteous. He thirsted to convince her of her sin,
and lead her to saving faith; and when He had done so
His desire was gratified.

I think I must have astonished some who have been
mourning and crying, "Oh, that the Lord would give me

to live upon His righteousness, and I would thank Him for ever and ever!" Why, you are one of the blessed. "Alas!" cries one, "I am pining to be delivered from sin —I do not mean from the punishment of it, sir, but from the taint of it; I want to be perfectly pure and holy." Do you? My dear friend, you are numbered among the blessed at this very moment.

III. And now I close with the best of all, *special satisfaction.* "Blessed are they which do hunger and thirst after righteousness: *for they shall be filled.*" This is a singular statement. They are to be blessed while they hunger and thirst; if they become filled, will they still be blessed? Yes, and what is more, they will still hunger and thirst. You say that is strange. Yes, it is; but everything is wonderful in the kingdom of God. Paradoxes, in spiritual things, are as plentiful as blackberries; in fact, if you cannot believe a paradox, you cannot believe in Christ Himself, for He is God and man in one person, and that is a paradoxical mystery. How can one person be infinite, and yet finite? How can He be immortal, and yet die? Ours is a Gospel wherein lieth many an orthodox paradox. He that is filled by Christ hungers more than he did before, only the hunger is of another kind, and has no bitterness in it. He that hungers most is the man who is full in the highest sense.

Now I am going to show you how it is that we can be filled even now, although still hungry and thirsty. For first, although we hunger and thirst after righteousness, *we are more than filled with the righteousness of God.* I do believe my God to be perfectly righteous, not only in His nature and essence, in His law and judgment, but also in all His decrees, acts, words and teachings. I sit me down, and anxiously peer into the dreadful truth of the eternal perdition of the wicked; but my heart is full of rest when I remember that God is righteous: the Judge of all the earth must do right. I cannot untie the knots of

difficulty over which some men stand perplexed, but I
know that God is righteous, and there I leave my be-
wilderments. God will see to it that the right thing is
done in every case, and for evermore.

Next, *we are also filled with the righteousness of Christ.*
What if I be sinful, what if I have no righteousness that
I dare bring before God? True, I have to cry with the
leper, "Unclean, unclean"; and yet, as a believer in the
Lord Jesus, I am justified in Him, accepted in Him, and
in Him complete.

Again, they that hunger and thirst after righteousness
are *filled with the righteousness which the Holy Spirit
works in them.* I do not say that they are satisfied to remain as they are, but they are grateful for what they are.
I am a sinner, but yet I do not love sin: is not this delightful? Though I have to fight daily against corruption,
yet I have received an inner life which will fight, and
must fight, and will not be conquered. If I have not yet
vanquished sin, it is something to be struggling against it.
Even now, by faith we claim the victory. "Thanks be to
God, which giveth us the victory through our Lord Jesus
Christ." Have you never felt as if you were full to the
brim, when you knew that you were "begotten again unto
a lively hope by the resurrection of Jesus Christ from the
dead"? Have you not been filled with delight to know
that you were no longer what you used to be, but that you
were now made a partaker of the divine nature, and elevated into the spiritual sphere, wherein you have fellowship with just men made perfect? Never despise what the
Holy Ghost has done for you, never under-value grace
already received; but, on the contrary, feel a divine delight, a filling-up of your heart, with what the Lord has
already done. Within your soul perfection lies in embryo:
all that you are yet to be is there in the seed. Heaven
slumbers in repentance, like an oak within an acorn. Glory
be to God for a new heart: glory be to God for life

from the dead! Here we are filled with thankfulness; and yet we go on hungering and thirsting that the blessing which God has given may be more fully enjoyed in our experience, and displayed in our life.

Brethren, I can tell you when again we get filled with righteousness, and that is when we see righteousness increasing among our fellowmen. The sight of one poor child converted has filled my heart for a week with joy unspeakable. I have talked frequently—with poor people who have been great sinners, and the Lord has made them great saints, and I have been as filled with happiness as a man could be. A dozen conversions have set all the bells of my heart ringing marriage-peals, and kept them at it by the month together. It is true that I might have remembered with sadness the multitudes of sinners who are still perishing, and this would have made me go on hungering and thirsting as I do; but still a score or two of conversions have seemed so rich a blessing that I have been filled with joy even to overflowing. Then have I felt like poor old Simeon, when he said, "Lord, now lettest Thou Thy servant depart in peace: for mine eyes have seen Thy salvation."

By-and-by we shall quit this mortal body, and we shall find ourselves in the disembodied state, "for ever with the Lord." We shall have no ears and eyes, but our spirit will discern and understand without these dull organs. Set free from this material substance, we shall know no sin. Soon will sound the resurrection trump, and the spirit will enter the refined and spiritualized body, and perfected manhood will be ours. Then the man will have his eyes, but they will never cast a lustful glance; he will have his ears, but they will never long for unclean talk, he will have his lips, but they will never lie; he will have a heart that will always beat truly and obediently: there will be nothing amiss within his perfect manhood. Oh, what a heaven that will be to us! I protest that I want no other heaven than to be with Christ, and to be like Him. Harps for music, and crowns for honor, are little as compared with the "kingdom of God and His righteousness."

My hearers, you will never be filled unless you hunger first. You must hunger and thirst here that you may be filled hereafter. If you are hungering and thirsting, what should you do? Look to Jesus, for He alone can satisfy you. Believe on our Lord Jesus Christ. Believe on Him now, for He is made of God unto us righteousness; and if you want righteousness you will find it in the Lord Jesus Christ, the only begotten Son of God.

CHAPTER FIVE

THE FIFTH BEATITUDE

"Blessed are the merciful: for they shall obtain mercy"— (Matthew 5:7).

Reading these Beatitudes as a whole, we see that this mercifulness is a characteristic which has grown out of the rest; it has sprung from all the previous works of grace, and the man is not merely merciful in the human sense, with a humanity which ought to be common to all mankind, but He is merciful in a higher and better sense, with a mercy which only the Spirit of God can ever teach to the soul of man.

Having noticed the rising of this Beatitude above the rest, we will now come to look at it more closely; and it is needful that we should be very guarded while speaking upon it; and in order to be so, we will ask, first, *Who are these blessed people?* Secondly, *What is their peculiar virtue?* And, thirdly, *What is their special blessing?*

I. *Who are these blessed people—the merciful that obtain mercy?*

First, *they were poor in spirit;* and it is no mean mercy to be emptied of our pride, to be brought to see how undeserving we are in the sight of God, and to be made to feel our personal weakness and want of everything that might make us fit for the presence of God. I could ask for some men whom I know no greater mercy than that they might be blessed with spiritual poverty, that they might be made to feel how poor they are, for they will never know Christ, and they will never rise to be practically merciful themselves till first they have seen their own true condition, and have obtained mercy enough to lie down at the foot of the Cross, and there, with a broken heart, to confess that they are empty and poor.

The connection also shows that these persons *had obtained mercy enough to mourn.* They had mourned over their past sins with bitter repentance, they had mourned over the conditions of practical alienation from God, into which sin had brought them, and they had mourned over the fact of their ingratitude to their Redeemer, and their rebellion against His Holy Spirit. They mourned because they could not mourn more, and wept because their eyes could not weep as they ought concerning sin.

They had also obtained the grace of meekness, and had become gentle, humble, contented, weaned from the world, submissive to the Lord's will, ready to overlook the offenses of others, having learned to pray, "Forgive us our debts, as we forgive our debtors"—no small blessing this.

They had obtained yet further grace, for *they had been taught to hunger and thirst after righteousness.* They had a spiritual appetite for the righteousness which is of God by faith. They had also a sacred hunger for the practical inwrought righteousness which is the work of the Spirit of God. They loved that which was right, and they hungered to do it; they hungered to see others do right, they hungered to see the kingdom of righteousness established, and the truth of God prevailing over all the earth. Was not this to obtain mercy indeed? And if out of this grew the character of being merciful, it was not to be ascribed to anything in themselves, or regarded as a natural outgrowth of their own disposition, but as another gift of grace, another fruit which grew out of special fruits which had already been given.

II. Now, secondly, *what is the peculiar virtue which is here ascribed to these blessed ones?* They were "merciful."

To be merciful would include, first of all, *kindness to the sons of want and the daughters of penury.* No merciful man could forget the poor. He who passed by their ills without sympathy, and saw their sufferings without relieving them, might prate as he would about inward grace, but grace in his heart there could not be. The Lord does not own as of His family one who can see his brother have need, and shut up "his bowels of compassion from him."

Next, *the merciful man has an eager eye, a weeping eye for mourners who are round about him.* The worst ill in the world is not poverty; the worst of ills is a depressed spirit; at least, I scarcely know anything that can be worse than this, and there are even among the excellent of the heart some who seldom have a bright day in the whole year. December seems to rule the whole twelve months. By reason of heaviness, they are all their life long subject to bondage. If they march to heaven, it is on crutches as Mr. Ready-to-halt did, and they water the way with tears as Miss Much-afraid did. They are afraid sometimes that they never were converted; at another time, that they have fallen from grace; at another time, that they have sinned the unpardonable sin; at another time, that Christ has gone from them, and they will never see His face again. They are full of all manner of troubles; "they reel to and fro, and stagger like a drunken man, and are often at their wits' end." There are many Christian people who always get out of the way of such folks as these; or if they come across them, they say, "It is enough to give anybody the miserables. Who wants to talk with such people? They ought not to be so sad; they really ought to be more cheerful; they are giving way to nervousness," and so on. That may be quite true, but it is always a pity to say it. You might as well tell a man when he has a headache that he is giving way to headache, or when he has the ague or the fever that he is giving way to the ague or the fever.

THE SERMON ON THE MOUNT

The fact is, there is nothing more real than some of those diseases which are traceable to the imagination, for they are real in their pain, though perhaps as to their causes we could not reason about them. The merciful man is always merciful to these people; he puts up with their whims; he knows that they are often foolish, but he understands that he would be foolish too if he were to tell them so, for it would make them more foolish than they are. Be ye merciful, even as your heavenly Father is merciful, toward those that are cast down.

This mercy extends itself next to the full forgiveness of all personal offences against ourselves. "Blessed are the merciful," that is, those persons who do not take to heart any injuries that are done them, any insults, intended or unintended. A certain governor of Georgia, in Mr. Wesley's day, said that he would have his servant on board his vessel flogged for drinking his wine; and when Mr. Wesley entreated that the man might be pardoned on that occasion, the governor said, "It is no use, Mr. Wesley; you know, sir, I never forgive." "Well, then, sir," said Mr. Wesley, "I hope you know that you will never be forgiven, or else I hope that you have never sinned." So, until we leave off sinning, we must never talk of not forgiving other people, for we shall need forgiveness for ourselves. "Blessed are the merciful," and such we mean to be.

But this mercifulness goes much further. *There must and will be great mercy in the Christian's heart toward those who are outwardly sinful.* The Pharisee had no mercy upon the man who was a publican. "Well," said he, "if he has gone down so low as to collect the Roman tax from his fellow-subjects, he is a disgraceful fellow. He may get as far as ever he can from my dignified self." And as for the harlot, it mattered not though she might be ready to shed enough tears to wash her Saviour's feet, yet she was a polluted thing; and Christ Himself was looked upon as being polluted because He suffered a

woman who had been a sinner thus to show her repentance and her love. Simon and the other Pharisees felt,
"Such people have put themselves out of the pale of society, and there let them keep. If they have gone astray
like that, let them suffer for it"; and there is much of that
spirit still in this hypocritical world, for a great part of
the world is a mass of the most awful hypocrisy that one
can imagine. There are men that are living in vile sin,
they know they are, and yet they go into society, and are
received as if they were the most respectable persons in
the world; but should it so happen that some poor person
is led astray—"Blessed are the merciful" who care for the
fallen, for those that have gone astray, "for they shall obtain mercy."

But *a genuine Christian has mercy on the souls of all
men.* He cares not merely for the extremely fallen class,
so called by the men of the world, but he regards
the whole race as fallen. He knows that all men have gone
astray from God, and that all are shut up in sin and unbelief till eternal mercy comes to their deliverance; therefore his pity goes forth toward the respectable, and the
rich, and the great, and he often pities princes and kings
because they have so few to tell them the truth. He
feels pity for them, and he feels pity for all nations—the
nations that sit in heathen darkness. He longs that grace
should come to all, and that the truths of the Gospel
should be proclaimed in every street, and Jesus made
known to every son and daughter of Adam; he has a love
for them all. And I pray you, brethren, never to trifle
with this true instinct of the new-born nature. The Christian man is merciful to all, and anxiously longs that they
may be brought to know the Saviour, and he makes efforts
to reach them; to the utmost of his ability, he tries to win
souls to Jesus. He also prays for them; if he is really a
child of God, he takes time to plead with God for sinners, and he gives what he can to help others to spend

their time in telling sinners the way of salvation, and
pleading with them as ambassadors for Christ. The Christian man makes this one of his great delights, if by any
means he may turn a sinner, by the power of the Spirit,
from the error of his ways, and so may save a soul from
death, and hide a multitude of sins.

Further, the merciful man shows his mercy to his
fellow-men in many other ways. *He is merciful to their
characters,* merciful in not believing a great many reports
he hears about reputed good men. It is a delightful thing
for Christians to have confidence in one another's characters. Wherever that rules in a church, it will prevent
a world of sorrow. It is for the Christian, at any rate,
not to expose, unless it be absolutely needful, as sometimes it is; but to deal ever toward the erring in the
gentlest manner possible.

And, brethren, we should be merciful to one another
in seeking never to look at the worst side of a brother's
character. Oh, how quick some are to spy out other people's faults!

You who are merciful will be ready to receive your
prodigal brother when he comes back to his Father's house.
Do not be like the elder brother, and when you hear the
music and the dancing ask, "What do these things mean?"
but count it meet that all should be glad when he who
was lost is found, he who was dead is made alive again.

I can only throw out hints that may suit one or another
of you. My brethren and sisters, we ought to be merciful
in the sense of *not allowing others to be tempted beyond
what they are able to bear.* You know that there is such
a thing as exposing our young people to temptation. Parents will sometimes allow their boys to start in life in
businesses where there is a chance of rising, but where
there is a greater chance of falling into great sin. They do
not esteem the moral risks which they sometimes run in
putting their sons into such a place where there is no re-

gard to morals and where there are a thousand nets of Satan spread to take unwary birds. Be merciful to your children; let them not be exposed to evils which were, perhaps, too strong for you in your youth, and which will
be too powerful for them. Let your mercy consider them,
and do not put them in that position.

And as to servants, we sometimes, when we have dishonest people about us, are about as guilty as they are.
We did not lock up our money, and take proper care of
it. If we had done so, they could not have stolen it. We
leave things about sometimes, and through our carelessness the suggestion may often come, "May I not take this
and that?" And so we may be partakers in their sins
through our own want of care. Remember, they are but
men and women, sometimes they are but boys and girls,
and do not put baits before them, do not play cat's paw
for Satan, but keep temptation from them as much as lieth
in you.

And let us be merciful, too, to people in not expecting
too much from them. I believe there are persons who expect those who work for them to toil four-and-twenty
hours a day, or thereabouts. No matter how hard the task,
it never strikes them that their servants' heads ache, or
that their legs grow weary. "What were they made for
but to slave for us?" That is the kind of notion some have,
but that is not the notion of a true Christian. He feels
that he desires his servants and his dependents to do their
duty, and he is grieved to find that many of them cannot
be led to do that; but when he sees them diligently doing
it, he often feels for them even more than they feel for
themselves, for he is considerate and gentle. Who would
wish to get out of his fellow-man that extra hour of work
which is just that which makes him wretched? Putting
all that I have said into one sentence, let us, dear friends,
be tender, considerate, kind and gentle to all.

"Oh!" says one, "if we were to go about the world

acting like that, we should get imposed upon, we should
get badly treated," and so on. Well, try it brother; try
it, sister; and you shall find that any misery that comes
to you through being too tender-hearted, and too gentle,
and too merciful, will be so light an affliction that it will
not be worthy to be compared with the peace of mind that
it will bring you, and the constant wellspring of joy which
it will put into your own bosom as well as into the bosoms
of others.

III. I shall close by briefly noticing *the blessing which is
promised to those who are merciful.*

It is said of them that "they shall obtain mercy." I
cannot help believing that this means in this present life
as well as in the life to come. Surely this is David's meaning in the forty-first Psalm: "Blessed is he that considereth
the poor; the Lord will deliver him in time of trouble . . .
He shall be blessed upon the earth." Is that text gone
altogether under the new dispensation? Are those promises
only meant for the old legal times? Ah, brethren, we have
the sun; but remember that, when the sun shines, the
stars are shining too; we do not see them by reason of
the greater brightness, but every star is shining in the day
as well as in the night, and increasing the light; and so,
though the greater promises of the Gospel do sometimes
make us forget the promises of the old dispensation, yet
they are not cancelled; they are still there, and they are
confirmed, and they are made yea and amen in Christ Jesus
unto the glory of God by us. I firmly believe that, when a
man is in trouble, if he has been enabled, through divine
grace, to be kind and generous toward others, he may look
to God in prayer, and say, "Lord, there is Thy promise; I
claim no merit for it, but Thy grace has enabled me,
when I saw others in the same condition as I am, to help
them. Lord, raise me up a helper." Job seemed to get
some comfort out of that fact; it is not our grandest comfort or our best; as I have said, it is not the sun, it is

only one of the stars. At the same time, we do not despise the starlight. I believe that God will full often help and bless in temporal matters those persons whom He has blessed with a merciful spirit toward others.

Often it is true in another sense that those who have been merciful obtain mercy, for they obtain mercy from others. Our Saviour said, "Give, and it shall be given unto you; good measure, pressed down, and shaken together, and running over, shall men give into your bosom. For with the same measure that ye mete withal it shall be measured to you again." There will be this sort of general feeling. If a man was sternly just, and no more, when he comes down in the world, few pity him; but that other man, whose earnest endeavor it was to be the helper of others, when he is found in trouble, all say, "We are so sorry for him."

But the full meaning of the text, no doubt, relates to that day of which Paul wrote concerning his friend, Onesiphorus, "The Lord grant unto him that he may find mercy of the Lord in that day." Do not think that I am preaching up mercy as a meritorious work; I did my best at the outset to put all that aside. But, as an evidence of grace, mercifulness is a prominent and distinguishing mark; and if you want proof of that, let me remind you that our Saviour's own description of the day of judgment runs thus, "Then shall the King say unto them on His right hand, Come, ye blessed of My Father, inherit the kingdom prepared for you from the foundation of the world: for I was an hungered, and ye gave Me meat: I was thirsty, and ye gave Me drink: I was a stranger, and ye took Me in: naked, and ye clothed Me: I was sick, and ye visited Me: I was in prison, and ye came unto Me." This, therefore, is evidence that they were blessed of the Father.

CHAPTER SIX

THE SIXTH BEATITUDE

"Blessed are the pure in heart: for they shall see God"—(Matthew 5:8).

It was a peculiarity of the great Apostle and High Priest of our profession, Jesus Christ our Lord and Saviour, that His teaching was continually aimed at the hearts of men. Other teachers had been content with outward moral reformation, but He sought the source of all the evil, that He might cleanse the spring from which all sinful thoughts, and words, and actions come. He insisted over and over again that, until the heart was pure, the life would never be clean. The memorable Sermon upon the Mount, from which our text is taken, begins with the benediction, "Blessed are the poor in spirit," for Christ was dealing with men's spirits—with their inner and spiritual nature. He did this more or less in all the Beatitudes, and this one strikes the center of the target as He says, not "Blessed are the pure in language, or the pure in action," much less "Blessed are the pure in ceremonies, or in raiment, or in food"; but "Blessed are the pure in *heart*." O beloved, whatever so-called "religion" may recognize as its adherent a man whose heart is impure, the religion of Jesus Christ will not do so. His message to all men still is, "Ye must be born again"; that is to say, the inner nature must be divinely renewed, or else you cannot enter or even see that kingdom of God which Christ came to set up in this world. If your actions should appear to be pure, yet, if the motive at the back of those actions should be impure, that will nullify them all. If your language should be chaste, yet, if your heart is reveling in foul imaginations, you stand before God not according to your words, but according to your desires; according to the set of the current of your affections, your real inward likes and dislikes, you shall be judged by Him. External purity is all that man asks at our hands, "for man looketh on the outward appearance, but the Lord looketh on the heart"; and the promises and blessings of the covenant of grace belong to those who are made pure in heart, and to none besides.

In looking upon this text, I want to show you, first, that *impurity of heart is the cause of spiritual blindness;* and, secondly that *the purification of the heart admits us to a most glorious sight:* "the pure in heart shall see God." Then I shall have to show you, in the third place, that the *purification of the heart is a divine operation,* which cannot be performed by ourselves, or by any human agency; but must be wrought by Him who is the thrice-holy Lord God of Sabaoth.

I. First, then, I have to remark that *impurity of heart is the cause of spiritual blindness*—the cause of a large part if not of all of it.

A man who is intoxicated cannot see clearly, his vision is often distorted or doubled; and there are other cups, besides those which intoxicate, which prevent the mental eye from having clear sight, and he who has once drunk deeply of those cups will become spiritually blind, and others, in proportion as they imbibe the noxious draughts, will be unable to see afar off.

There are moral beauties and immoral horrors which certain men cannot see because they are impure in heart. Take, for instance, the covetous man, and you will soon see that there is no other dust that blinds so completely as gold dust. There is a trade which many regard as bad from top to bottom; but if it pays the man who is engaged in it, and he is of a grasping disposition, it will be almost impossible to convince him that it is an evil trade. You will usually find that the covetous man sees no charm in generosity. He thinks that the liberal man, if he is not actually a fool, is so near akin to one that he might very easily be mistaken for one. He himself admires that which can be most easily grasped; and the more of it that he can secure, the better is he pleased. There are innumerable things that a man cannot see if he holds a coin over each of his eyes; he cannot even see the sun then; and if he keeps the gold over his eyes, he will become blind. The pure in heart can see; but when covetousness gets into the heart, it makes the eye dim or blind.

The same thing may be said with regard to spiritual truth as well as moral truth. We frequently meet with persons who say that they cannot understand the Gospel of Christ. At the bottom, in nine cases out of ten, I believe that it is their sin which prevents their understanding it.

The great central doctrine of the atonement can never be fully appreciated until a man's heart is rectified. You have probably often heard such remarks as these, "I don't see why there should be any recompense made to God for sin. Why could He not forgive transgression at once, and have done with it? What need is there of a substitutionary sacrifice?" Ah, sir! if you had ever felt the weight of sin upon your conscience, if you had ever learned to loathe the very thought of evil, if you had been broken-hearted because you have been so terribly defiled by sin, you would feel that the atonement was not only required by God, but that it was also required by your own sense of justice; and instead of rebelling against the doctrine of a vicarious sacrifice, you would open your heart to it, and cry, "That is precisely what I need." The purest-hearted people who have ever lived are those who have rejoiced to see God's righteous law vindicated and magnified by Christ's death upon the Cross as the Substitute for all who believe in Him, so that while God's mercy is displayed in matchless majesty, intensest satisfaction is felt that there could be a way of reconciliation by which every attribute of God should derive honor and glory, and yet poor lost sinners should be lifted up into the high and honorable position of children of God. The pure in heart see no difficulty in the atonement; all the difficulties concerning it arise from the want of purity there.

The same may be said of the equally-important truth of regeneration. The impure in heart cannot see any need of being born again. They say, "We admit that we are not quite all that we should be, but we can easily be made all right. As to the talk about a new creation, we do not see any need of that. We have made some few mistakes, which will be rectified by experience; and there have been some errors of life which we trust may be condoned by future watchfulness and care." But if the unrenewed man's heart were pure, he would see that his nature had been an evil thing from the beginning; and he would realize that thoughts of evil as naturally rise in us as sparks do from a fire, and he would feel that it would be a dreadful thing that such a nature as that should remain unchanged.

There is one form of impurity which, beyond all others, seems to blind the eye to spiritual truth, and that is duplicity of heart. A man who is simple-minded, honest, sincere, childlike, is the man who enters the kingdom of heaven when its door is opened to him. The things of the kingdom are hidden from the double-minded and the deceitful, but they are plainly revealed to the babes in grace —the simple-hearted, transparent people who wear their heart upon their sleeve. It is quite certain that the hypocrite will never see God while he continues in his hypocrisy. In fact, he is so blind that he cannot see anything, and certainly cannot see himself as he really is in God's sight. The man who is quite satisfied with the name of a

Christian without the life of a Christian will never see
God nor anything at all until his eyes are divinely opened.
What does it matter to anyone else what his opinion is
upon any subject whatever? We should not care to have
praise from the man who is double-minded, and who is
practically a liar; for, while he is one thing in his heart,
he endeavors to pass himself off for another thing in his
life.

The crafty man, too, never sees God. I am afraid for
no man so much as for the crafty, the man whose guiding
star is "policy." I have seen rough sailors converted to
God, and blasphemers, harlots and great sinners of almost
all kinds brought to the Saviour, and saved by His grace;
and often they have told the honest truth about their
sins, and have blurted out the sad truth in an outspoken
fashion; and when they have been converted, I have often
thought that they were like the good ground of which our
Saviour spoke, with an honest and good heart in spite of
all their badness. But as for the men of snakelike nature,
who say to you, when you talk to them about religion,
"Yes, yes," but do not mean it at all—the men who are
never to be trusted, Mr. Smoothtongue, Mr. Facingboth-
ways, Mr. Byends, Mr. Fairspeech, and all that class of
people, God Himself never seems to do anything but let
them alone; and, so far as my observation goes, His grace
seldom seems to come to these double-minded men who
are unstable in all their ways. These are the people who
never see God.

I think there are some Christians who never see God so
well as others do—I mean some brethren who, from their
peculiar constitution, seem naturally of a questioning spirit.
They are generally puzzled about some doctrinal point or
other, and their time is mostly taken up with answering
objections and removing doubts. Perhaps some poor humble countrywoman, who sits in the aisle, and who knows,
as Cowper says, nothing more than that her Bible is true,

and that God always keeps His promises, sees a great deal more of God than the learned and quibbling brother who vexes himself about foolish questions to no profit.

II. Our second remark was that *the purification of the heart admits us to a most glorious sight*: "The pure in heart *shall see God.*"

What does that mean? It means many things; I will briefly mention some of them. First, *the man, whose heart is pure, will be able to see God in nature.* When his heart is clean, he will hear God's footfall everywhere in the garden of the earth in the cool of the day. He will hear God's voice in the tempest, sounding in peal on peal from the tops of the mountains. He will behold the Lord walking on the great and mighty waters, or see Him in every leaf that trembles in the breeze. Once get the heart right, and then God can be seen everywhere. To an impure heart, God cannot be seen anywhere; but to a pure heart God is to be seen everywhere, in the deepest caverns of the sea, in the lonely desert, in every star that gems the brow of midnight.

Further, *the pure in heart see God in the Scriptures.* Impure minds cannot see any trace of God in them; they see reasons for doubting whether Paul wrote the Epistle to the Hebrews, they doubt the canonicity of the Gospel according to John, and that is about all that they ever see in the Bible; but the pure in heart see God on every page of this blessed Book. As they read it devoutly and prayerfully, they bless the Lord that He has been pleased so graciously to reveal Himself to them by His Spirit, and that He has given them the opportunity and the desire to enjoy the revelation of His holy will.

Beside that, *the pure in heart see God in His Church.* The impure in heart cannot see Him there at all. To them, the Church of God is nothing but a conglomeration of divided sects; and looking upon these sects, they can see nothing but faults, and failures, and imperfections. It should always be remembered that every man sees that which is according to his own nature. When the vulture soars in the sky, he sees the carrion wherever it may be; and when the dove on silver wings mounts up to the azure, she sees the clean winnowed corn wherever it may be. The lion sees his prey in the forest, and the lamb sees its food in the grassy meadow. Unclean hearts see little or nothing of good among God's people, but the pure in heart see God in His Church, and rejoice to meet Him there.

But seeing God means much more than perceiving traces of Him in nature, in the Scriptures, and in His Church; it means that *the pure in heart begin to discern something of God's true character.* Any man who is caught in a thunderstorm, and who hears the crash of the thunder, and sees what havoc the lightning flashes work, perceives that God is mighty. If he is not so foolish as to be an atheist, he says, "How terrible is this God of the lightning and the thunder!" But to perceive that God is eternally just and yet infinitely tender, and that He is sternly severe and yet immeasurably gracious, and to see the various attributes of the Deity all blending into one another as the colors of the rainbow make one harmonious and beautiful whole—this is reserved for the man whose eyes have been first washed in the blood of Jesus, and then anointed with heavenly eye-salve by the Holy Spirit. It is only such a man who sees that God is always and altogether good, and who admires Him under every aspect, seeing that all His attributes are beautifully blended and balanced, and that each one sheds additional splendor upon all the rest. The pure in heart shall in that sense see God, for they shall appreciate His attributes and understand His character as the ungodly never can.

But, more than that, *they shall be admitted into His fellowship.* When you hear some people talk about there being no God, and no spiritual things, and so on, you need not be at all concerned at what they say, for they are not

in a position to warrant them in speaking about the matter. For instance, an ungodly man says, "I do not believe
there is a God, for I never saw Him." I do not doubt the
truth of what you say; but when I tell you that I *have*
seen Him, you have no more right to doubt my word than
I have to doubt yours.

And, lastly, *the time shall come when those who have
thus seen God on earth shall see Him face to face in
heaven.* Oh, the splendor of that vision! It is useless for
me to attempt to talk about it. Possibly, within a week,
some of us will know more about it than all the divines
on earth could tell us. 'Tis but a thin veil that parts us
from the glory-world.

III. Now, lastly, and very briefly, I have to remind you
that *this purification of the heart is a divine work.*

And, believe me when I tell you that *it is never an un-
necessary work.* No man (except the man Christ Jesus)
was ever born with a pure heart; all have sinned, all
need to be cleansed, there is none good; no, not one.

Neither can the heart be purified *by any process of outward reformation.* The attempt has often been made to
work from the outside to the inside, but it cannot be done;
you might as well try to give a living heart to a marble
statue by working upon the outside of it with a mallet
and chisel; and to make a sinner pure in heart is as great
a miracle as if God were to make that marble statue live,
and breathe, and walk.

The heart can only be purified by God's Holy Spirit.
He must come upon us, and overshadow us, and when He
thus comes to us, then is our heart changed, but never before that. When the Spirit of God thus comes to us, He
cleanses the soul—to follow the line of our Saviour's teaching in the chapter before us—by showing us our spiritual
poverty: "Blessed are the poor in spirit." That is the
first work of God's grace—to make us feel that we are

poor, that we are nothing, that we are undeserving, ill-deserving, hell-deserving sinners.

As the Spirit of God proceeds with His work, the next thing that He does is to make us mourn; "Blessed are they that mourn." We mourn to think that we should have sinned as we have done, we mourn after our God, we mourn after pardon; and then the great process that effectually cleanses the heart is the application of the water and the blood which flowed from the riven side of Christ upon the Cross. Here it is, O sinners, that ye will find a double cure from the guilt and from the power of sin! When faith looks to the bleeding Saviour, it sees in Him not merely pardon for the past, but the putting away of the sinfulness of the present. The angel said to Joseph, before Christ was born, "Thou shalt call His name Jesus: for He shall save His people from their sins." The whole process of salvation may be briefly explained thus. The Spirit of God finds us with foul hearts, and He comes and throws a divine light into us so that we see that they are foul. Then He shows us that, being sinners, we deserve to endure God's wrath, and we realize that we do. Then He says to us, "But that wrath was borne by Jesus Christ for you." He opens our eyes, and we see that "Christ died for us"—in our room, and place, and stead. We look to Him, we believe that He died as our Substitute, and we trust ourselves with Him. Then we know that our sins are forgiven us for His name's sake, and the joy of pardoned sin goes through us with such a thrill as we never felt before; and the next moment the forgiven sinner cries, "Now that I am saved, now that I am pardoned, my Lord Jesus Christ, I will be Thy servant for ever. I will put to death the sins that put Thee to death; and if Thou wilt give me the strength to do so, I will serve Thee as long as I live!"

The current of the man's soul ran before toward evil; but the moment that He finds that Jesus Christ died for

him, and that his sins are forgiven him for Christ's sake,
the whole stream of his soul rushes in the other direction
toward that which is right; and though he still has a
struggle against his old nature, yet, from that day forth
the man is pure in heart; that is to say, his heart loves
purity, his heart seeks after holiness, his heart pines after
perfection.

Now he is the man who sees God, loves God, delights in
God, longs to be like God, and eagerly anticipates the time
when he shall be with God, and see Him face to face.
That is the process of purification; may you all enjoy it
through the effectual working of the Holy Spirit! If you
are willing to have it, it is freely proclaimed to you. If
you truly desire the new heart and the right spirit, they
will be graciously given to you. There is no need for you
to try to fit yourselves to receive them. God is able to
work them in you this very hour. He who will wake the
dead with one blast of the resurrection trumpet can change
your nature with the mere volition of His gracious mind.
He can create in you a new heart, renew a right spirit
within you. The power of the Holy Spirit to renew the
human heart is boundless. "Oh," says one, "would that
He would renew my heart, that He would change my nature!" If that is your heart's desire, send up that prayer
to heaven now. Let not the wish die in your soul, but turn
it into a prayer, and then breathe it out unto God, and
hearken to what God has to say to you. It is this: "Come
now, and let us reason together, saith the Lord: though
your sins be as scarlet, they shall be as white as snow;
though they be red like crimson, they shall be as wool";
or this: "Believe on the Lord Jesus Christ, and thou shalt
be saved"—saved from thy love of sin, saved from thy old
habits, and so completely saved that thou shalt become
one of the pure in heart who see God.

Chapter Seven

THE PEACEMAKER

"Blessed are the peacemakers; for they shall be called the children of God" (Matthew 5:9).

Now let us endeavor to enter into the meaning of our text. First, let us *describe the peacemaker;* secondly, let us *proclaim his blessedness;* thirdly, let us *set him to work;* and then, fourthly, *let the preacher become a peacemaker himself.*

I. First, *let us describe the peacemaker.* The peacemaker, while distinguished by his character, has the outward position and condition of other men. He stands in all relations of life just as other men do.

Thus the peacemaker is a *citizen,* and though he be a Christian, he remembers that Christianity does not require him to forego his citizenship, but to use and to improve it for Christ's glory. The peacemaker, then, as a citizen, loves peace.

But the peacemaker is not only a citizen, but *a man,* and if sometimes he leaves general politics alone, yet as a man he thinks that the politics of his own person must always be those of peace. There, if his honor be stained, he standeth not up for it; he counteth that it were a greater stain to his honor for him to be angry with his fellow than for him to bear an insult. He heareth others say, "If you tread upon a worm it will turn"; but he saith, "I am not a worm, but a Christian, and therefore I do not turn, except to bless the hand that smites, and to pray for those that despitefully use me." He has his temper, for the peacemaker can be angry, and woe to the man who cannot be; he is like Jacob halting on his thigh, for anger is one of the holy feet of the soul, when it goes in the right direction; but while he can be angry he learns to "be angry and sin not," and "he suffereth not the sun to go down upon his wrath." When he is at home, the peacemaker seeks to be quiet with his servants and with his household; he puts up with many things sooner than he will speak one uncomely word, and if he rebukes, it is ever with gentleness, saying, "Why do ye this?—why do ye this?"—not with the severity of a judge, but with the tenderness of a father.

The peacemaker *goes abroad* also, and when he is in company he sometimes meets with slurs, and even with insults, but he learns to bear them, for he remembers that Christ endured much contradiction of sinners against Himself. The peacemaker does not rush to defend himself, knowing that He whom he serves will take care that his good name will be preserved, if only he himself be careful how he walks among men.

And then the peacemaker is a *neighbor,* and though he never seeks to meddle with his neighbor's dispute, more especially if it be a dispute between his neighbor and his wife, for well he knows that if they two disagree, yet they will both agree very soon to disagree with him, if he meddles between them; if he be called in when there is a dispute between two neighbors, he never excites them to animosity, but he says to them, "Ye do not well, my brethren; wherefore strive ye with one another?" And though he takes not the wrong side, but seeks ever to do justice, yet he tempers ever his justice with mercy, and says unto the one who is wronged, "Canst not thou have the nobility to forgive?"

But once again, the peacemaker has it for his highest title, that he is *a Christian.* Being a Christian he unites himself with some Christian church; and here, as a peace-

maker, he is as an angel of God. Even among churches
there be those that are bowed down with infirmities, and
these infirmities cause Christian men and Christian women
to differ at times. So the peacemaker says, "This is un-
seemly, my brother; let us be at peace"; and he remembers what Paul says, "I beseech Euodias, and I beseech
Syntyche, that they be of the same mind in the Lord"; and
he thinks that if these two were thus besought by Paul
to be of the same mind, unity must be a blessed thing,
and he labors for it. And sometimes the peacemaker, when
he sees differences likely to arise between his denomina-
tion and others, turns to the history of Abram, and he reads
how the herdsmen of Abram did strive with the herdsmen of Lot, and he notes that in the same verse it is said,
"And the Canaanite and the Perizzite dwelled then in the
land." So he thinks it was a shame that where there were
Perizzites to look on, followers of the true God should disagree. He says to Christians, "Do not this, for we make
the devil sport; we dishonor God; we damage our own
cause; we ruin the souls of men"; and he says, "Put up
your swords into your scabbards; be at peace and fight
not one with another." They who be not peacemakers,
when received into a church, will fight upon the smallest
crotchet; will differ about the minutest point; and we have
known churches rent in pieces, and schisms committed
in Christian bodies through things so foolish, that a wise
man could not perceive the occasion; things so ridiculous,
that a reasonable man must have overlooked them. The
peacemaker says, "Follow peace with all men." Specially
he prays that the Spirit of God, who is the Spirit of peace,
might rest upon the church at all times, binding believers
together in one, that they being one in Christ, the world
may know that the Father hath sent His Son into the
world; heralded as His mission was with an angelic
song—"Glory to God in the highest; on earth peace, good
will toward men."

Now, I trust in the description which I have given of the peacemaker, I may have described some of you; but I fear the most of us would have to say, "Well, in many things I come short."

II. Having thus described the peacemaker, I shall go on to *declare His blessedness*. "Blessed are the peacemakers: for they shall be called the children of God." A three-fold commendation is implied.

First, he is blessed; that is, God blesses him, and I wot that he whom God blesses, is blessed; and he whom God curses, is cursed. God blesses him from the highest heavens; God blesses him in a god-like manner; God blesses him with the abundant blessings which are treasured up in Christ.

While he is blessed of God, the blessedness is diffused through his own soul. His conscience bears witness that as in the sight of God through the Holy Spirit, he has sought to honor Christ among men. More especially is he most blessed when he has been most assailed with curses; for then the assurance greets him, "So persecuted they the prophets that were before you." And whereas he has a command to rejoice at all times, yet he finds a special command to be exceedingly glad when he is ill-treated. Therefore, he takes it well, if for well-doing he be called to suffer, and he rejoices thus to bear a part of the Saviour's cross. He goes to his bed; no dreams of enmity disturb his sleep; he rises and goes to his business, and he fears not the face of any man. Loving all, he is thus peaceful in his own soul, and he is blessed as one that inherits the blessing of the Most High.

Not infrequently it comes to pass that he is even blessed by the wicked; for though they would withhold a good word from him, they cannot. Overcoming evil with good, he heaps coals of fire upon their heads, and melts the coldness of their enmity, till even they say, "He is a good man." And when he dies, those whom he has made at peace with one another, say over his tomb, " 'Twere well if the world should see many of his like; there were not half the strife, nor half the sin in it, if there were many like to him."

Secondly, you will observe that the text not only says he is blessed; but it adds, that *he is one of the children of God.* This he is by adoption and grace; but peacemaking is a sweet evidence of the work of the peaceful Spirit within. As the child of God, moreover, he has a likeness to his Father who is in heaven. God is peaceful, longsuffering and tender, full of lovingkindness, pity and compassion. So is this peacemaker. Being like unto God, he bears his Father's image. Thus does he testify to men that he is one of God's children. As one of God's children, the peacemaker has access to his Father. He goes to Him with confidence, saying, "Our Father which art in heaven," which he dare not say unless he could plead with a clear conscience, "Forgive us our debts, as we forgive our debtors." He feels the tie of brotherhood with man, and therefore he feels that he may rejoice in the Fatherhood of God. He comes with confidence and with intense delight to his Father who is in heaven, for he is one of the children of the Highest, who does good both to the unthankful and to the evil.

And still, there is a third word of commendation in the text. "They shall be *called* the children of God." They not only are so, but they shall be called so. That is, even their enemies shall call them so; even the world shall say, "Ah! that man is a child of God." Perhaps, beloved, there is nothing that so strikes the ungodly as the peaceful behavior of a Christian under insult.

III. But now, in the third place, I am to try and *set the peacemaker to work.*

Ye have much work to do, I doubt not, in your own household and your own circles of acquaintance. Go and do it. You remember well that text in Job—"Can that which is unsavory be eaten without salt? or is there any taste in the white of an egg?"—by which Job would have us know, that unsavory things must have something else with them, or else they will not well be pleasant for food. Now, our religion is an unsavory thing to men: we must put salt with it; and this salt must be our quietness and peacemaking disposition. Then they who would have eschewed our religion alone, will say of it, when they see the salt with it, "This is good," and they will find some relish in this "white of an egg." If you would commend your godliness to the sons of men, in your own houses make clear and clean work, purging out the old leaven, that ye may offer sacrifice to God of a godly and heavenly sort. If ye have any strifes among you, or any divisions, I pray you, even as God, for Christ's sake, forgave you, so also do ye. By the bloody sweat of Him who prayed for you, and by the agonies of Him who died for you, and in dying said, "Father, forgive them, for they know not what they do," forgive your enemies, "pray for them that despitefully use you, and bless them that curse you." Let it be always said of you, as a Christian, "That man is meek and lowly in heart, and would sooner bear injury himself then cause an injury to another."

But the chief work I want to set you about is this, Jesus Christ was the greatest of all peace-makers. "He is our Peace." He came to make peace with Jew and Gentile, "for He hath made both one, and hath broken down the middle wall of partition between us." He came to make peace between all striving nationalities, for we are "no more Greek, barbarian, Scythian, bond nor free, but Christ is all in all." He came to make peace between His Father's justice and our offending souls, and He hath made peace for us through the blood of His Cross. Now, ye who are the sons of peace, endeavor as intruments in His hands to make peace between God and men. For your children's souls let your earnest prayers go up to heaven.

For the souls of all your acquaintance and kinsfolk let your supplications never cease. Pray for the salvation of your perishing fellow creatures. Thus will you be peace-makers. And when you have prayed, use all the means within your power. Preach, if God has given you the ability; preach with the Holy Ghost sent down from heaven—the reconciling word of life. Teach, if you cannot preach. Teach the Word. "Be instant in season and out of season." "Sow beside all waters"; for the Gospel "speak-eth better things than the blood of Abel," and cries peace to the sons of men. Write to your friends of Christ; and if you cannot speak much, speak a little for Him. But oh! make it the object of your life to win others for Christ. Never be satisfied with going to heaven alone. Ask the Lord that you may be the spiritual father of many chil-dren, and that God may bless you to the ingathering of much of the Redeemer's harvest.

IV. The minister has now, in the last place, *to practice his own text, and endeavor through God the Holy Spirit to be a peacemaker.*

I speak to many a score of persons who know nothing of peace; for "There is no peace, saith my God, to the wicked." "The wicked is like the troubled sea, which can-not rest, whose waters cast up mire and dirt." I speak not to you with any desire of making a false peace with your souls. Woe to the prophets who say "Peace, peace, when there is no peace!" Rather, let me, first of all, that we may make sound work in this matter, expose the peace-less, the warring state of your soul.

O soul! thou art at war with thy conscience. Thou hast tried to quiet it, but it *will* prick thee. Oh, there be some of you to whom conscience is as a ghost, haunting you by day and night. Ye know the good, though ye choose the evil; ye prick your fingers with the thorns of con-science when ye try to pluck the rose of sin. To you the downward path is not an easy one; it is hedged up and ditched up, and there be many bars and gates and chains on the road; but ye climb over them, determined to ruin your own souls.

But more, there is war between thee and God's law. The ten commandments are against thee. The first comes forward and says, "Let him be cursed, for he denies Me. He has another God besides Me, his God is his belly, he yieldeth homage to his lust." All the ten commandments, like ten great pieces of cannon, are pointed at thee today, for you have broken all God's statutes, and lived in the daily neglect of all His commands. Soul! thou wilt find it a hard thing to go to war with the law. When the law came in peace, Sinai was altogether on a smoke, and even Moses said, "I do exceedingly fear and quake." What will ye do when the law comes in terror, when the trumpet of the archangel shall tear you from your grave, when the eyes of God shall burn their way into your guilty soul, when the great books shall be opened, and all your sin and shame shall be punished? Can you stand against an angry law in that day?

But, sinner, do you know that you are at war with God? He that made thee and was your best friend you have forgotten and neglected. He has fed you, and you have used your strength against Him. He has clothed you—the clothes you have upon your back today are the livery of His goodness—yet, instead of being the servant of Him whose livery you wear, you are the slave of His greatest enemy. The very breath in your nostrils is the loan of His charity, and yet you use that breath perhaps to curse Him, or at the best, in lasciviousness or loose conversation, to do dishonor to His laws. He that made you has become your enemy through your sin, and you are still today hating Him and despising His Word. You say, "I do not hate Him." Soul, I charge you then, "Believe in the Lord Jesus Christ." "No," say you, "I cannot, I will not do that!" Then you hate Him. If you loved Him, you would keep this His great command. "His commandment is not grievous," it is sweet and easy. You would believe in His Son if you did love the Father, for "he that loveth the Father loveth Him also that is begotten of Him."

This, then, is the state of every unconverted man and woman. You are at war with conscience, at war with God's law, and at war with God Himself. And, now, then, as God's ambassadors, we come to treat of peace. I beseech you give heed. "As though God did beseech you by me, I pray you, in Christ's stead, be ye reconciled to God." "In His stead." Let the preacher vanish for a moment. Look and listen. It is Christ speaking to you now. Methinks I hear Him speak to some of you. This is the way He speaks, "Soul, I love you; I love you from My heart; I would not have you at enmity with My Father." The tear proves the truth of what He states, while He cries, "How often would I have gathered you, as a hen gathereth her chickens under her wing, but ye would not." "Yet," says He, "I come to treat with you of peace. Come, now, and let us reason together. I will make an everlasting covenant with you, even the sure mercies of David." "Sinner," says He, "thou art bidden now to hear God's note of peace to thy soul, for thus it runs—'Thou art guilty and condemned; wilt thou confess this? Art thou willing to throw down thy weapons now, and say, Great God, I yield, I yield; I would no longer be Thy foe?'" If so, peace is proclaimed to you. "Let the wicked forsake his way, and the unrighteous man his thoughts, and let him turn unto the Lord, for He will have mercy upon him, and to our God, for He will abundantly pardon." Pardon is freely presented to every soul that unfeignedly repents of its sin; but that pardon must come to you through faith.

So Jesus stands, points to the wounds upon His breast, and spreads His bleeding hands. He says, "Sinner, trust in Me and live!" God proclaims to you no longer His fiery

law, but His sweet, His simple gospel, believe and live.
"He that believeth on the Son is not condemned; but he
that believeth not is condemned already, because he hath
not believed in the name of the only begotten Son of
God." "As Moses lifted up the serpent in the wilderness,
even so must the Son of Man be lifted up, that whosoever
believeth on Him should not perish, but have eternal life."
O soul! does the Spirit of God move in you? Do you say,
"Lord, I would be at peace with Thee?" Are you willing
to take Christ on His own terms, and they are no terms
at all—they are simply that you should make no terms
in the matter, but give yourself up, body, soul and spirit,
to be saved of Him? Now, if my Master were here visibly,
I think He would plead with you in such a way that many
of you would say, "Lord, I believe, I would be at peace
with Thee." But even Christ Himself never converted a
soul apart from the Holy Spirit, and even He as a preacher
won not many to Him, for they were hard of heart. If
the Holy Ghost be here, He may as much bless you when
I plead in Christ's stead as though He pleaded Himself.
Soul! Will you have Christ or not? Young men, young
women; you may never hear this word preached in your
ears again. Will you die at enmity against God?

Cast thyself before His dear cross, and say—
    "A guilty, weak, and helpless worm,
        Into Thy arms I fall;
    Be thou my strength and righteousness,
        My Jesus and my all."

If He rejects you, tell us of it. If He refuses you, let us
hear it. There was never such a case yet. He always has
received those that come. He always will. He is an open-
handed and an open-hearted Saviour. O sinner! God bring
you to put your trust in Him once for all!

CHAPTER EIGHT

THE FATHERHOOD OF GOD

"Our Father which art in heaven"—(Matthew 6:9).

I think there is room for great doubt, whether our Saviour intended the prayer, of which our text forms a part, to be used in the manner in which it is commonly employed among professing Christians. It is the custom of many persons to repeat it as their morning prayer, and they think that when they have repeated these sacred words they have done enough. I believe that this prayer was never intended for universal use. Jesus Christ taught it not to all men, but to His disciples, and it is a prayer adapted only to those who are the possessors of grace, and are truly converted. In the lips of an ungodly man it is entirely out of place. Does one say, "Ye are of your father the devil, for his works ye do?" Why, then, should you mock God by saying, "Our Father which art in heaven." For how can He be your Father? Have you two Fathers?

I much question also, whether this prayer was intended to be used by Christ's own disciples as a constant form of prayer. It seems to me that Christ gave it as a model, whereby we are to fashion all our prayers, and I think we may use it to edification, and with great sincerity and earnestness, at certain times and seasons. I have seen an architect form the model of a building he intends to erect of plaster or wood; but I never had an idea that it was intended for me to live in. I have seen an artist trace on a piece of brown paper, perhaps, a design which he intended afterwards to work out on more costly stuff; but I never

imagined the design to be the thing itself. This prayer
of Christ is a great chart, as it were: but I cannot cross the
sea on a chart. It is a map; but a man is not a traveler
because he puts his finger across the map. And so a man
may use this form of prayer, and yet be a total stranger
to the great design of Christ in teaching it to His disciples.
I feel that I cannot use this prayer to the omission of
others. Great as it is, it does not express all I desire to
say to My Father which is in heaven. There are many
sins which I must confess separately and distinctly; and
the various other petitions which this prayer contains require, I feel, to be expanded, when I come before God in
private; and I must pour out my heart in the language
which His Spirit gives me; and more than that, I must
trust in the Spirit to speak the unutterable groanings of
my spirit, when my lips cannot actually express all the
emotions of my heart. Let none despise this prayer; it
is matchless, and if we must have forms of prayer, let
us have this first, foremost and chief; but let none think
that Christ would tie His disciples to the constant and
only use of this. Let us rather draw near to the throne of
the heavenly grace with boldness, as children coming to a
father, and let us tell forth our wants and our sorrows
in the language which the Holy Spirit teaches us.

And now, coming to the text, there are several things
we shall have to notice here. And first, I shall dwell upon
the double relationship mentioned: "Our Father which art
in heaven." There is *sonship*—"Father"; there is *brotherhood,* for it says, *"Our* Father"; and if He be the common
Father of us, then we must be brothers; for there are two
relationships, sonship and brotherhood. In the next place,
I shall utter a few words upon the spirit which is necessary to help us before we are able to utter this—*The
spirit of adoption,* whereby we can cry, "Our Father which
art in heaven." And then, thirdly, I shall conclude with
the double argument of the text, for it is really an argu-

ment upon which the rest of the prayer is based. "Our
Father which art in heaven," is, as it were, a strong argument used before supplication itself is presented.

I. First, *the double relationship implied in the text.*

We take the first one. Here is *sonship*—"Our Father
which art in heaven." How are we to understand this,
and in what sense are we the sons and daughters of
God? Some say that the Fatherhood of God is universal,
and that every man, from the fact of His being created
by God, is necessarily God's son, and that therefore every
man has a right to approach the throne of God, and say,
"Our Father which art in heaven." To that I must demur.
I believe that in this prayer we are to come before God,
looking upon Him not as our Father through creation,
but as our Father through adoption and the new birth.
I will briefly state my reasons for this.

I have never been able to see that creation necessarily
implies fatherhood. I believe God has made many things
that are not His children. Has He not made the heavens
and the earth, the sea and the fulness thereof? And are
they His children? You say these are not rational and in-
telligent beings; but He made the angels, who stand in an
eminently high and holy position, are they His children?
"Unto which of the angels said He at any time, thou art
My son?" I do not find, as a rule, that angels are called
the children of God; and I must demur to the idea that
mere creation brings God necessarily into the relationship
of a Father. Does not the potter make vessels of clay?
But is the potter the father of the vase, or of the bottle?
No, beloved, it needs something beyond creation to con-
stitute the relationship, and those who can say, "Our Father which art in heaven," are something more than
God's creatures: they have been adopted into His family.
He has taken them out of the old black family in which
they were born; He has washed them, and cleansed them,
and gives them a new name and a new spirit, and made

them "heirs of God, and joint-heirs with Christ"; and all
this of His own free, sovereign, unmerited, distinguishing
grace.

. Having adopted them to be His children, He has, in the
next place, *regenerated them by the Spirit of the living
God*. He has "begotten them again unto a lively hope,
by the resurrection of Jesus Christ from the dead," and
no man has a right to claim God as his Father, unless he
feels in his soul, and believes, solemnly, through the faith
of God's election, that he has been adopted into the one
family of God which is in heaven and earth, and that
he has been regenerated or born again.

This relationship also involves *love*. If God be my
Father, He loves me. And, oh, how He loves me! When
God is a Friend, He is the best of friends, and sticketh
closer than a brother; and when He is a Father He is the
best of fathers. O fathers! perhaps you do not know
how much you love your children. When they are sick
you find it out, for you stand by their beds and you
pity them, as their little frames are writhing in pain.
Well, "like as a father pitieth his children, so the Lord
pitieth them that fear Him." You know how you love
your children, too, when they grieve you by their sin; anger arises, and you are ready to chasten them, but no
sooner is the tear in their eye, than your hand is heavy, and
you feel that you had rather smite yourself than smite
them; and every time you smite them you seem to cry, "Oh,
that I should have thus to afflict my child for his sin!
Oh, that I could suffer in his stead!" And God, even our
Father, "doth not afflict willingly." Is not that a sweet
thing? He is, as it were, compelled to it; even the Eternal
arm is not willing to do it; it is only His great love and
deep wisdom that brings down the blow.

But if this sonship involves the love of God to us, it
involves also, the duty of *love to God*. Oh! heir of heaven,
if you are God's child, will you not love your Father?

What son is there that loves not his father? Is he not less than human if he loves not his sire? Let his name be blotted from the book of remembrance that loves not the woman that brought him forth, and the father that begat him. And we, the chosen favorites of heaven, adopted and regenerated, shall not we love Him?

Furthermore, if we say "Our Father which art in heaven," we must recollect that our being sons involves the duty of *obedience to God*. When I say "My Father," it is not for me to rise up and go in rebellion against His wishes; if He be a father, let me note His commands, and let me reverentially obey; if He has said "Do this," let me do it, not because I dread Him, but because I love Him; and if He forbids me to do anything, let me avoid it. There are some persons in the world who have not the spirit of adoption, and they can never be brought to do a thing unless they see some advantage to themselves in it; but with the child of God, there is no motive at all; he can boldly say, "I have never done a right thing since I have followed Christ because I hoped to get to heaven by it, nor have I ever avoided a wrong thing because I was afraid of being damned." For the child of God knows his good works do not make him acceptable to God, for he was acceptable to God by Jesus Christ long before he had any good works; and the fear of hell does not affect him, for he knows that he is delivered from that, and shall never come into condemnation, having passed from death unto life. He acts from pure love and gratitude, and until we come to that state of mind, I do not think there is such a thing as virtue; for if a man has done what is called a virtuous action because he hoped to get to heaven or to avoid hell by it, whom has he served? Has he not served himself? And what is that but selfishness? But the man who has no hell to fear and no heaven to gain, because heaven is his own and hell he never can enter, that man is capable of virtue.

The second tie of the text is *brotherhood*. It does not say *my* Father, but *our* Father. Then it seems there are a great many in the family.

"Our Father." When you pray that prayer, remember you have a good many brothers and sisters that do not know their Father yet, and you must include them all; for all God's elect ones, though they be uncalled as yet, are still His children, though they know it not. In one of Krummacher's beautiful little parables there is a story like this:

"Abraham sat one day in the grove at Mamre, leaning His head on his hand, and sorrowing. Then his son Isaac came to him, and said, 'My father, why mournest thou? what aileth thee?' Abraham answered and said, 'My soul mourneth for the people of Canaan, that they know not the Lord, but walk in their own ways, in darkness and foolishness.' 'Oh, my father,' answered the son, 'is it only this? Let not thy heart be sorrowful; for are not these their own ways?' Then the patriarch rose up from his seat, and said, 'Come now, follow me,' And he led the youth to a hut, and said to him, 'Behold.' There was a child which was imbecile, and the mother sat weeping by it. Abraham asked her, 'Why weepest thou?' Then the mother said, 'Alas, this my son eateth and drinketh, and we minister unto him, but he knows not the face of his father, nor his mother. Thus his life is lost, and this source of joy is sealed to him.'"

Is not that a sweet little parable, to teach us how we ought to pray for the many sheep that are not yet of the fold, but which must be brought in? We ought to pray for them, because they do not know their Father. Christ has bought them, and they do not know Christ; the Father has loved them from before the foundation of the world, and yet they know not the face of their Father. When you say "Our Father," think of the many of your brothers and sisters that are in the back streets, that are in the

dens and caves of Satan. Think of your poor brother that
is intoxicated with the spirit of the devil; think of him,
led astray to infamy, and lust, and perhaps to murder, and
in your prayer pray for them who know not the Lord.

"Our Father." That, then, includes those of God's children who differ from us in their doctrine. Ah! there are
some that differ from us as wide as the poles; but yet they
are God's children. Some time ago at a prayer-meeting
I called upon two brothers in Christ to pray one after another, the one a Wesleyan and the other a strong Calvinist,
and the Wesleyan prayed the most Calvinistic prayer of
the two, I do believe—at least, I could not tell which was
which. I listened to see if I could not discern some peculiarity even in their phraseology; but there was none.
"Saints in prayer appear as one"; for when they get on
their knees, they are all compelled to say "Our Father,"
and all their language afterwards is of the same sort.

When you pray to God, put in the poor; for is He not
the Father of many of the poor, rich in faith, and heirs of
the kingdom, though they be poor in this world. Come,
my sister, if you bow your knee amid the rustling of silk
and satin, yet remember the cotton and the print. My
brother, is there wealth in your hand, yet I pray you,
remember your brethren of the horny hand and the dusty
brow; remember those who could not wear what you
wear, nor eat what you eat, but are as Lazarus compared
with you, while you are as Dives. Pray for them; put
them all in the same prayer, and say "Our Father."

And pray for those that are divided from us by the sea—
those that are in heathen lands, scattered like precious
salt in the midst of this world's putrefaction. Pray for
all that name the name of Jesus, and let your prayer be a
great and comprehensive one. "Our Father, which art in
heaven." And after you have prayed that, rise up and
act it. Say not "Our Father," and then look upon your
brethren with a sneer or a frown. I beseech you, live like

a brother, and act like a brother. Help the needy; cheer
the sick; comfort the faint-hearted; go about doing good;
minister unto the suffering people of God, wherever you
find them, and let the world take knowledge of you, that
you are when on your feet what you are upon your knees
—that you are a brother unto all the brotherhood of
Christ, a brother born for adversity, like your Master Himself.

II. Having thus expounded the double relationship
I will go on to another important part of the subject,
namely, *the spirit of adoption.*

I am extremely puzzled and bewildered how to explain
to the ungodly what is the spirit with which we must
be filled, before we can pray this prayer. There is a name-
less charm there; we cannot describe or understand it:
it is a sacred touch of nature, a throb in the breast that
God has put there, and that cannot be taken way. The
fatherhood is recognized by the childship of the child.
And what is that spirit of a child—that sweet spirit that
makes him recognize and love his father? I cannot tell
you unless you are a child yourself, and then you will
know. And what is "the spirit of adoption, whereby we
cry Abba, Father?" I cannot tell you; but if you felt it
you will know it. It is a sweet compound of faith that
knows God to be my Father, love that loves Him as
my Father, joy that rejoices in Him as my Father, fear
that trembles to disobey Him because He is my Father,
and a confident affection and trustfulness that relies upon
Him, and casts itself wholly upon Him, because it knows
by the infallible witness of the Holy Spirit, that Jehovah,
the God of earth and heaven, is the Father of my heart.
Oh! have you ever felt the spirit of adoption? There is
nought like it beneath the sky. Save heaven itself there
is nought more blissful than to enjoy that spirit of adoption. Oh! when the wind of trouble is blowing, and waves
of adversity are rising, and the ship is reeling to the rock,

how sweet then to say "My Father," and to believe that
His strong hand is on the helm!—when the bones are ach-
ing, and when the loins are filled with pain, and when
the cup is brimming with wormwood and gall, to say "My
Father," and seeing that Father's hand holding the cup
to the lip, to drink it steadily to the very dregs, because
we can say, "My Father, not my will, but Thine be done."

My readers, have you the spirit of adoption? If not,
you are miserable men. May God Himself bring you to
know Him! May He teach you your need of Him! May
He lead you to the Cross of Christ, and help you to look
to your dying Brother! May He bathe you in the blood
that flowed from His open wounds, and then, accepted in
the Beloved, may you rejoice that you have the honor to
be one of that sacred family.

III. And now, in the last place, I said that there was in
the title, *a double argument.* "Our Father." That is,
"Lord, hear what I have got to say. Thou art my Father."
If I come before a judge I have no right to expect that he
shall hear me at any particular season in aught that I
have to say. If I came merely to crave for some boon or
benefit to myself, if the law were on my side, then I could
demand an audience at his hands; but when I come as a
law-breaker, and only come to crave for mercy, or for
favors I deserve not, I have no right to expect to be heard.
But a child, even though he is erring, always expects his
father will hear what he has to say. "Lord, if I call Thee
King Thou wilt say, 'Thou art a rebellious subject; get
thee gone.' If I call thee Judge Thou wilt say, 'Be still,
or out of thine own mouth will I condemn thee.' If I
call Thee Creator Thou wilt say unto me, 'It repenteth Me
that I made man upon the earth.' If I call Thee my Pre-
server Thou wilt say unto me, 'I have preserved thee, but
thou hast rebelled against Me.' But if I call Thee Father,
all my sinfulness doth not invalidate my claim. If Thou
be my Father, then Thou lovest me; if I be Thy child,

then Thou wilt regard me, and poor though my language be, Thou wilt not despise it."

As one dear brother said the other day at the prayer meeting. He could not get on in prayer, and he finished up on a sudden by saying "Lord, I cannot pray tonight as I should wish; I cannot put the words together; Lord, take the meaning, take the meaning," and sat down. That is just what David said once, "Lo, all my desire is before Thee"—not my words, but my desire, and God could read it. We should say, "Our Father," because that is a reason why God should hear what we have to say.

But there is another argument. "Our Father." "Lord give me what I want." If I come to a stranger, I have no right to expect he will give it me. He may out of his charity; but if I come to a father, I have a claim, a sacred claim. My Father, I shall have no need to use arguments to move Thy bosom; I shall not have to speak to Thee as the beggar who crieth in the street: for because Thou art my Father Thou knowest my wants, and Thou art willing to relieve me. It is Thy business to relieve me; I can come confidently to Thee, knowing Thou wilt give me all I want. If we ask our Father for anything when we are little children, we are under an obligation certainly; but it is an obligation we never feel. If you were hungry and your father fed you, would you feel an obligation as you would if you went into the house of a stranger? You go into a stranger's house trembling, and you tell him you are hungry. Will he feed you? He says yes, he will give you somewhat; but if you go to your father's table, almost without asking, you sit down as a matter of course, and feast your fill, and you rise and go, and feel you are indebted to him; but there is not a grievous sense of obligation. Now, we are all deeply under obligation to God, but it is a child's obligation—an obligation which impels us to gratitude, but which does not constrain us to feel that we have been demeaned by it. Oh!

if He were not my Father, how could I expect that He
would relieve my wants? But since He is my Father, He
will, He must hear my prayers, and answer the voice of
my crying, and supply all my needs out of the riches of
His fulness in Christ Jesus the Lord.

Has your father treated you badly lately? I have this
word to you, then; your father loves you quite as much
when he treats you roughly as when he treats you kindly.
There is often more love in an angry father's heart than
there is in the heart of a father who is too kind. Give me
a father that is angry with my sins, and that seeks to
bring me back, even though it be by chastisement. Thank
God you have a Father that can be angry, but that loves
you as much when He is angry as when He smiles upon
you.

Go away with that upon your mind, and rejoice. But if
you love not God and fear Him not, go home, I beseech
you, to confess your sins, and to seek mercy through the
blood of Christ; and may this message be made useful in
bringing you into the family of Christ, though you have
strayed from Him long: and though His love has followed
you long in vain, may it now find you, and bring you to
His house rejoicing!

CHAPTER NINE

A HEAVENLY PATTERN FOR OUR EARTHLY LIFE

"Thy will be done in earth, as it is in heaven"
—(Matthew 6:10).

If the prayer of our text had not been dictated by the Lord Jesus Himself, we might think it too bold. Can it ever be that this earth, a mere drop of a bucket, should touch the great sea of life and light above and not be lost in it? Can it remain earth and yet be made like to heaven? Will it not lose its individuality in the process? This earth is subject to vanity, dimmed with ignorance, defiled with sin, furrowed with sorrow; can holiness dwell in it as in heaven? Our Divine Instructor would not teach us to pray for impossibilities; He puts such petitions into our mouths as can be heard and answered. Yet certainly this is a great prayer; it has the hue of the infinite about it. Can earth be tuned to the harmonies of heaven? Has not this poor planet drifted too far away to be reduced to order and made to keep rank with heaven? Is it not swathed in mist too dense to be removed? Can its grave-clothes be loosed? Can Thy will, O God, be done in earth as it is in heaven? It can be, and it must be; for a prayer wrought in the soul by the Holy Spirit is ever the shadow of a coming blessing, and He that taught us to pray after this manner did not mock us with vain words. It is a brave prayer, which only a heaven-born faith can utter; yet it is not the offspring of presumption, for presumption never longs for the will of the Lord to be perfectly performed.

I. May the Holy Spirit be with us, while I first lead
you to observe that *the comparison is not far-fetched.*
That our present obedience to God should be like to that
of holy ones above is not a strained and fanatical notion.
It is not far-fetched, *for earth and heaven were called into
being by the same Creator.* The empire of the Maker com-
prehends the upper and the lower regions. "The heaven,
even the heavens are the Lord's"; and "the earth is the
Lord's, and the fulness thereof." He sustaineth all things
by the word of His power both in heaven above and in
the earth beneath. Jesus reigneth both among angels and
men, for He is Lord of all.

Meanwhile, remember also that *there is an analogy between earth and heaven,* so that the one is the type of the
other. You could not describe heaven except by borrowing
the things of earth to symbolize it; and this shows that
there is a real likeness between them. What is heaven?
It is Paradise, or a garden. Walk amid your fragrant
flowers and think of heaven's bed of spices. Heaven is a
kingdom: thrones, and crowns, and palms are the earthly
emblems of the heavenlies. Heaven is a city; and there,
again, you fetch your metaphor from the dwelling-places
of men. It is a place of "many mansions"—the homes of
the glorified. Houses are of earth, yet is God our dwelling-place. Heaven is a wedding-feast; and even such is
this present dispensation. The tables are spread here as
well as there; and it is our privilege to go forth and
bring in the hedge-birds and the highwaymen, that the
banqueting-hall may be filled. While the saints above
eat bread in the marriage supper of the Lamb, we do the
like below in another sense.

Between earth and heaven there is but a thin partition.
The home country is much nearer than we think. I question if "the land that is very far off" be a true name for
heaven. Was it not an extended kingdom on earth which

was intended by the prophet rather than the celestial home? Heaven is by no means the far country, for it is the Father's house. Are we taught to say, "Our Father which art in heaven"? Where the Father is the true spirit of adoption counts itself near. Our Lord would have us mingle heaven with earth by naming it twice in this short prayer. See how He makes us familiar with heaven by mentioning it next to our usual food, making the next petition to be, "Give us this day our daily bread." This does not look as if it should be thought of as a remote region. Heaven is, at any rate, so near that in a moment we can speak with Him that is King of the place, and He will answer to our call. A little while and we shall see our Lord. Perhaps another day's march will bring us within the city gate. And what if another fifty years of life on earth should remain, what is it but the twinkling of an eye?

Clear enough is it that the comparison between the obedience of earth and that of heaven is not far-fetched. If heaven and heaven's God be, in truth, so near to us, our Lord has set before us a homely model taken from our heavenly dwelling-place. The petition only means— let all the children of the one Father be alike in doing His will.

II. Secondly, *this comparison is eminently instructive.* Does it not teach us that *what* we do for God is not everything, but *how* we do it is also to be considered? The Lord Jesus Christ would not only have us do the Father's will, but do it after a certain model. And what an elevated model it is! Yet is it none too elevated, for we would not wish to render to our heavenly Father service of an inferior kind. If none of us dare say that we are perfect, we are yet resolved that we will never rest until we are. If none of us dare hope that even our holy things are without a flaw, yet none of us will be satisfied while a

spot remains upon them. We would give to our God the
utmost conceivable glory.

"Thy will *be done* in earth, as it is in heaven." Mark
the words *"be done,"* for they touch a vital point of the
text. God's will is *done* in heaven. How very practical!
On earth His will is often forgotten, and His rule ignored.
In the church of the present age there is a desire to be
doing something for God, but few inquire what He wills
them to do. Many things are done for the evangelizing of
the people which were never commanded by the great
Head of the Church, and cannot be approved of by Him.
Can we expect that He will accept or bless that which
He has never commanded? Will-worship is as sin in His
sight. We are to do His will in the first place, and then
to expect a blessing upon the doing of that will. Would
God His will were not alone preached and sung below,
but actually done as it is in heaven.

In heaven the will of God is done *in spirit,* for they are
spirits there. It is done *in truth* with undivided heart,
and unquestioned desire. On earth, too often, it is done
and yet not done; for a dull formality mocks real obedience. Here obedience often shades off into dreary rou-
tine. We sing with the lips, but our hearts are silent.
We pray as if the mere utterance of words were prayer.

III. Thirdly, I beg you to notice, dear friends, that
*this comparison of holy service on earth to that which
is in heaven, is based upon facts.* The facts will both
comfort and stimulate us. Two places are mentioned
in the text which seem very dissimilar, and yet the
likeness exceeds the unlikeness—earth and heaven.

Brethren, we are in the same company below as they
enjoy above. Up there they are with Christ, and here
He is with us, for He hath said — "Lo, I am with you
alway, even unto the end of the world." There is a
difference as to the brightness of His presence; but not

as to the reality of it. Thus you see we are partakers of
the same privileges as the shining ones within the city
gates. The church below is a chamber of the one great
house, and the partition which separates it from the
church above is a mere veil, of inconceivable thinness.
Wherefore should we not do the Lord's will on earth as
it is done in heaven?

"But heaven is a place of peace," says one; "there they
rest from their labors." Beloved, our estate here is not
without its peace and rest. "Alas," cries one, "I find it
far otherwise." I know it. But whence come wars and
fightings but of our fretfulness and unbelief? "We which
have believed do enter into rest." That is not in all respects a fair allegory which represents us as crossing
the Jordan of death to enter into Canaan. No, my
brethren, believers are in Canaan now; how else could
we say that the Canaanite is still in the land? We have
entered upon the promised heritage, and we are warring
for the full possession of it. We have peace with God
through Jesus Christ our Lord. Brethren, having rest
already, and being participators of the joy of the Lord,
why should we not serve God on earth as they do in
heaven?

"But we have not their victory," cries one, "for they
are more than conquerors." Yes, and "our warfare is
accomplished." We have prophetic testimony to that fact.
Moreover, "This is the victory that overcometh the world,
even our faith." In the Lord Jesus Christ the Lord giveth
us the victory, and maketh us to triumph in every place.
We are warring; but we are of good cheer, for Jesus
has overcome the world, and we also overcome by His
blood. Ever is this our war-cry, "Victory! Victory!" The
Lord will tread Satan under our feet shortly. Why should
we not do the Lord's will on earth as it is done in heaven?

Heaven is the place of fellowship with God, and this

is a blessed feature in its joy; but in this we are now participators, for "Truly our fellowship is with the Father, and with His Son Jesus Christ." The fellowship of the Holy Ghost is with us all; it is our joy and our delight. Having communion with the triune God, Father, Son, and Holy Spirit, we are uplifted and sanctified, and it is becoming that by us the will of the Lord should be done on earth as it is in Heaven.

IV. Lastly, *this comparison*, which I feel I can so feebly bring out, of doing the will of God on earth as it is done in heaven, *ought to be borne out by holy deeds*. Here is the urgency of the missionary enterprise. God's will can never be intelligently done where it is not known; therefore, in the first place, *it becomes us as followers of Jesus to see to it that the will of the Lord is made known* by heralds of peace sent forth from among us. Why has it not been already published in every land? We cannot blame the great Father, nor impute the fault to the Lord Jesus. The Spirit of the Lord is not straitened, nor the mercy of God restrained. Is it not probably true that the selfishness of Christians is the main reason for the slow progress of Christianity? If Christianity is never to spread in the world at a more speedy rate than the present, it will not even keep pace with the growth of the population. If we are going to give to Christ's kingdom no larger a percentage than we have usually given, I suppose it will require about an eternity-and-a-half to convert the world; or, in other words, it will never be done.

Our text, dear friends, leads me to say that as God's will must be known that it may be done, *it must be God's will that we should make it known;* because God is love, and the law under which He has placed us is that we love. What love of God dwelleth in that man who denies to be a benighted heathen that light without which he will be lost? Love is a grand word to talk of, but it is nobler as a principle to be obeyed. Can there be love of God in that man's heart who will not help to send the Gospel to those who are without it? We want to bless the world; we have a thousand schemes by which to bless it, but if ever God's will is done in earth as it is done in heaven it will be an unmixed and comprehensive blessing. This is the one balm for all earth's wounds. They will bleed still until the Christ shall come to bind them up. Oh, let us then, since this is the best thing that can be, show our love to God and man by spreading His saving truth.

Oh, brothers, let us live as we shall wish we had lived when life is over; let us fashion a life which will bear the light eternal. Is it life to live otherwise? Is it not a sort of fainting fit, a coma, out of which life may not quite have gone, but all that is worth calling life has oozed away? Unless we are striving mightily to honor Jesus, and bring home His banished, we are dead while we live. Let us aim at a life which will outlast the fires which shall try every man's work.

CHAPTER TEN

"LEAD US NOT INTO TEMPTATION"

"Lead us not into temptation"—(Matthew 6:13).

In trying to commend this prayer to you, let us notice, first of all, *the spirit which suggests such a petition;* secondly, *the trials which such a prayer deprecates;* and then, thirdly, *the lessons which it teaches.*

I. *What suggests such a prayer as this?* — "Lead us not into temptation."

First, from the position of the clause, I gather, by a slight reasoning process, that it is suggested by *watchfulness.* This petition follows after the sentence, "Forgive us our debts." I will suppose the petition to have been answered, and the man's sin is forgiven. What then? If you will look back upon your own lives you will soon perceive what generally happens to a pardoned man, for "As in water face answereth to face, so the heart of man to man." One believing man's inner experience is like another's, and your own feelings were the same as mine. Soon after the penitent has received forgiveness and has the sense of it in his soul, he is tempted of the devil, for Satan cannot bear to lose his subjects, and when he sees them cross the border line and escape out of his hand he gathers up all his forces and exercises all his cunning if, perchance, he may slay them at once. To meet this special assault the Lord makes the heart watchful. Perceiving the ferocity and subtlety of Satan's temptations, the new-born believer, rejoicing in the perfect pardon he has received, cries to God, "Lead us not into temptation." It is the fear of losing the joy of pardoned sin which thus cries out to the good Lord — "Our Father, do not suffer us to lose the salvation we have so lately obtained. Do not even subject it to jeopardy. Do not permit Satan to break our new-found peace. We have but newly escaped, do not plunge us in the deeps again. Swimming to shore, some on boards and some on broken pieces of the ship, we have come safe to land; constrain us not to tempt the boisterous main again. Cast us not upon the rough billows any more. O God we see the enemy advancing; he is ready if he can to sift us as wheat. Do not suffer us to be put into his sieve, but deliver us, we pray Thee."

It is a prayer of watchfulness; and mark you, though we have spoken of watchfulness as necessary at the commencement of the Christian life, it is equally needful even to the close. There is no hour in which a believer can afford to slumber. Watch, I pray you, when you are alone, for temptation, like a creeping assassin, has its dagger for solitary hearts. You must bolt and bar the door well if you would keep out the devil. Watch yourself in public, for temptations in troops cause their arrows to fly by day. The choicest companions you can select will not be without some evil influence upon you unless you be on your guard. Remember our blessed Master's words, "What I say unto you I say unto all, Watch."

Next, it seems to me to be the natural prayer *of holy horror at the very thought of falling again into sin.* It were better for us to die at once than to live on and return to our first estate and bring dishonor upon the name of Jesus Christ our Lord. The prayer before us springs from the shrinking of the soul at the first approach of the tempter. The footfall of the fiend falls on the startled ear of the timid penitent: he quivers like an aspen leaf,

and cries out, What, is he coming again? And is it possible that I may fall again? And may I once more defile
these garments with that loathsome murderous sin which
slew my Lord? "O my God," the prayer seems to say,
"keep me from so dire an evil. Lead me, I pray Thee,
where Thou wilt—ay, even through death's dark valley,
but do not lead me into temptation, lest I fall and dishonor thee." The burnt child dreads the fire. He who
has once been caught in the steel trap carries the scars
in his flesh and is horribly afraid of being again held
by its cruel teeth.

The third feeling, also, is apparent; namely, *diffidence
of personal strength.* The man who feels himself strong
enough for anything is daring, and even invites the battle
which will prove his power. "Oh," says he, "I care not:
they may gather about me who will; I am quite able to
take care of myself and hold my own against any number."
He is ready to be led into conflict, he courts the fray. Not
so the man who has been taught of God and has learned
his own weakness; he does not want to be tried, but
seeks quiet places where he may be out of harm's way.
Put him into the battle and he will play the man, let
him be tempted and you will see how steadfast he will be;
but he does not ask for conflict, as, methinks, few soldiers
will who know what fighting means. Surely it is only
those who have never smelled gunpowder, or seen the
corpses heaped in bloody masses on each other, that are
so eager for the shot and shell, but your veteran would
rather enjoy the piping times of peace. No experienced
believer ever desires spiritual conflict, though perchance
some raw recruits may challenge it. In the Christian
a recollection of his previous weakness—his resolutions
broken, his promises unkept—makes him pray that he
may not in future be severely tested. He does not dare
to trust himself again. He wants no fight with Satan, or

with the world; but he asks that if possible he may be kept from those severe encounters, and his prayer is, "Lead us not into temptation." The wise believer shows a sacred diffidence—nay, I think I may say an utter despair of himself: and even though he knows that the power of God is strong enough for anything, yet is the sense of his weakness so heavy upon him that he begs to be spared too much trial. Hence the cry, "Lead us not into temptation."

Once more, do you not think that this prayer breathes the spirit of *confidence*—confidence in God? "Why," says one, "I do not see that." To me—I know not whether I shall be able to convey my thought—to me there is a degree of tender familiarity and sacred boldness in this expression. Of course, God will lead me now that I am His child. Moreover, now that He has forgiven me, I know that He will not lead me where I can come to any harm. This my faith ought to know and believe, and yet for several reasons there rises to my mind a fear lest His providence should conduct me where I shall be tempted. Is that fear right or wrong? It burdens my mind; may I go with it to my God? May I express in prayer this misgiving of soul? May I pour out this anxiety before the great, wise, loving God? Will it not be impertinent? No, it will not, for Jesus puts the words into my mouth and says, "After this manner pray ye." You are afraid that He may lead you into temptation; but He will not do so; or should He see fit to try you, He will also afford you strength to hold out to the end. He will be pleased in His infinite mercy to preserve you. Where He leads it will be perfectly safe for you to follow, for His presence will make the deadliest air to become healthful. But since instinctively you have a dread lest you should be conducted where the fight will be too stern and the way too rough, tell it to your heavenly Father without reserve. That is the way to keep up love and confidence. So if you have a suspicion in your soul that mayhap thy Father might put you into temptation too strong for you, tell it to Him. Tell it to Him, though it seems taking a great liberty. Though the fear may be the fruit of unbelief yet make it known to your Lord, and do not harbor it sullenly. Remember the Lord's prayer was not made for Him, but for you, and therefore it reads matters from your standpoint and not from His.

Our Lord's prayer is not for our Lord; it is for us, His children; and children say to their fathers ever so many things which it is quite proper for them to say, but which are not wise and accurate after the measure of their parents' knowledge. Their father knows what their hearts mean, and yet there may be a good deal in what they say which is foolish or mistaken. So I look upon this prayer as exhibiting that blessed childlike confidence which tells out to its father a fear which grieves it, whether that fear be altogether correct or no. Whenever you have a fear of any kind, hurry off with it to Him who loves His little ones, and like a father pities them and soothes even their needless alarms.

Thus have I shown that the spirit which suggests this prayer is that of watchfulness, of holy horror at the very thought of sin, of diffidence of our own strength, and of confidence in God.

II. Secondly, let us ask, *what are these temptations which the prayer deprecates?* or say rather, what are these trials which are so much feared?

I do not think the prayer is intended at all to ask God to spare us from being afflicted for our good, or to save us from being made to suffer as a chastisement. Of course we should be glad to escape those things; but the prayer aims at another form of trial, and may be paraphrased thus —"Save me, O Lord, from such trials and sufferings as may lead me into sin. Spare me from too great trials, lest I fall by their overcoming my patience, my faith, or my steadfastness.

Now, as briefly as I can, I will show you how men may be led into temptation by the hand of God.

And the first is *by the withdrawal of divine grace.* Suppose, dear friends—you who walk in the light of God's countenance and bear life's yoke so easily because He sustains you—suppose His presence were withdrawn from you, what must be your portion? We are all so like to Samson in this matter that I must bring him in as the illustration, though he has often been used for that purpose by others. So long as the locks of our head are unshorn we can do anything and everything: we can rend lions, carry gates of Gaza, and smite the armies of the alien. It is by the divine consecrating mark that we are strong in the power of His might; but if the Lord be once withdrawn and we attempt the work alone, then are we weak as the tiniest insect. When the Lord hath departed from thee, O Samson, what art thou more than another man? Then the cry, "the Philistines be upon thee, Samson," is the knell of all thy glory. Thou dost vainly shake those lusty limbs of thine. Now thou wilt have thine eyes put out and the Philistines will make sport of thee. In view of a like catastrophe we may well be in an agony of supplication. Pray then, "Lord, leave me not; and lead me not into temptation by taking Thy Spirit from me."

Another set of temptations will be found in *providential conditions.* The words of Agar, the son of Jaken, shall be my illustration here. "Remove far from me vanity and lies; give me neither poverty nor riches; feed me with food convenient for me; lest I be full, and deny Thee, and say, Who is the Lord? or lest I be poor, and steal, and take the name of my God in vain." Some of us have never known what actual want means, but have from our youth up lived in social comfort. Ah, dear friends, when we see what extreme poverty has made some men do, how do we know that we should not have behaved even worse if we had been as sorely pressed as they? We may well shudder and say, "Lord, when I see poor families crowded together in one little room where there is scarcely space to observe common decency; when I see hardly bread enough to keep the children from crying for hunger; when I see the man's garments wearing out upon his back, and by far too thin to keep out the cold; I pray thee subject me not to such trial, lest if I were in such a case I might put forth my hand and steal. Lead me not into the temptation of pining want."

And, on the other hand, look at the temptations of money when men have more to spend than they can possibly need, and there is around them a society which tempts them into racing, and gambling, and whoredom, and all manner of iniquities. The young man who has a fortune ready to hand before he reaches years of discretion, and is surrounded by flatterers and tempters all eager to plunder him; do you wonder that he is led into vice, and becomes a ruined man morally? Like a rich galleon waylaid by pirates, he is never out of danger; is it a marvel that he never reaches the port of safety? Women tempt him, men flatter him, vile messengers of the devil fawn upon him, and the young simpleton goes after them like an ox to the slaughter, or as a bird hasteth to the snare and knoweth not that it is for his life. You may very well thank heaven you never knew the temptation, for if it were put in your way you would also be in sore peril. If riches and honor allure you, follow not eagerly after them, but pray, "Lead us not into temptation."

Providential positions often try men. There is a man much pushed for ready money in business; how shall he meet that heavy bill? If he does not meet it there will

be desolation in his family; his place of business will be
broken up; everyone will be ashamed of him, his children
will be outcasts, and he will be ruined. He has only to
use a sum of trust money; he has no right to risk a penny
of it, for it is not his, but still by its temporary use he
may perchance tide over the difficulty. The devil tells him
he can put it back in a week. If he does touch that money
it will be an evil action, but then he says, "Nobody will
be hurt by it, and it will be a wonderful accommodation,"
and so on. If he yields to the suggestion, and the thing
goes right, there are some who would say, "Well, after
all, there was not much harm in it, and it was a prudent
step, for it saved him from ruin." But if it goes wrong,
and he is found out, then everyone says, "It was a shame-
ful robbery. The man ought to be transported." But,
brethren, the action was wrong in itself, and the conse-
quences neither make it better nor worse. Do not bitterly
condemn, but pray again and again, "Lead us not into
temptation. Lead us not into temptation." You see God
does put men into such positions in providence at times
that they are severely tried. It is for their good that they
are tried, and when they can stand the trial they magnify
His grace, and they themselves become stronger men: the
test has beneficial uses when it can be borne, and God
therefore does not always screen His children from it.

There are temptations, too, arising out of *physical conditions*. There are some men who are moral in character
because they are in health; and there are other men who
are bad, who, I do not doubt, if we knew all about them,
should have some little leniency shown them, because
of the unhappy conformation of their constitution. Why,
there are many people to whom to be cheerful and
to be generous is no effort whatsoever, while there are
others who need to labor hard to keep themselves from

despair and misanthropy. Diseased livers, palpitating hearts and injured brains are hard things to struggle against. Does that poor old lady complain? She has only had the rheumatism thirty years, and yet she now and then murmurs! How would you be if you felt her pains for thirty minutes?

So, again, *mental conditions* often furnish great temptations. When a man becomes depressed he becomes tempted. Those among us who rejoice much often sink about as much as we rise, and when everything looks dark around us Satan is sure to seize the occasion to suggest despondency. God forbid that we should excuse ourselves, but, dear brother, pray that you be not led into this temptation. Perhaps if you were as much a subject of nervousness and sinking of spirit as the friend you blame for his melancholy, you might be more blameworthy than he, therefore, pity rather than condemn.

On the other hand, when the spirits are exhilarated and the heart is ready to dance for joy, it is easy for levity to step in and for words to be spoken amiss. Pray the Lord not to let you rise so high nor sink so low as to be led into evil. "Lead us not into temptation," must be our hourly prayer.

Further than this, there are temptations arising out of *personal associations*, which are formed for us in the order of providence. We are bound to shun evil company, but there are cases in which, without fault on their part, persons are made to associate with bad characters. I may instance the pious child whose father is a swearer, and the godly woman lately converted, whose husband remains a swearer and blasphemes the name of Christ. It is the same with workmen who have to labor in workshops, where lewd fellows at every half-a-dozen words let fall an oath, and pour forth that filthy language which shocks us every day more and more. Well, if persons are obliged to work in such shops, or to live in such families there may come times when under the lash of jest and sneer and sarcasm the heart may be a little dismayed and the tongue may refuse to speak for Christ. Such a silence and cowardice are not to be excused, yet do not censure thy brother, but say, "Lord, lead me not into temptation." How know you that you would be more bold? Peter quailed before a talkative maid, and you may be cowed by a woman's tongue. The worst temptation for a young Christian that I know of is to live with a hypocrite — a man so sanctified and demure that the young heart, deceived by appearances, fully trusts him while the wretch is false at heart and rotten in life. And such wretches there are who, with the pretence and affectation of sanctimoniousness, will do deeds at which we might weep tears of blood: young people are frightfully staggered, and many of them become deformed for life in their spiritual characteristics through associating with such beings as these. When you see faults caused by such common but horrible causes, say to yourself, "Lord, lead me not into temptation. I thank thee for godly parents and for Christian associations and for godly examples; but what might I have been if I had been subjected to the very reverse? If evil influences had touched me when like a vessel I was upon the wheel, I might have exhibited even grosser failings than those which I now see in others."

Thus I might continue to urge you to pray, dear friends, against various temptations; but let me say, the Lord has for some men *special tests*, such as may be seen in the case of Abraham. He gives him a son in his old age, and then says to him, "Take now thy son, thine only son, Isaac, whom thou lovest, and offer him for a burnt-offering." You will do right to pray, "Lord, lead me not into such a temptation as that. I am not worthy to be so tried.

Oh do not so test me." I have known some Christians to
sit down and calculate whether they could have acted as
the patriarch did. It is very foolish, dear brother. When
you are called upon to do it you will be enabled to make
the same sacrifice by the grace of God, but if you are
not called upon to do it, why should the power be given?
Shall God's grace be left unused? Your strength shall be
equal to your day, but it shall not exceed it. I would have
you ask to be spared the sterner tests.

To put my meaning in a way in which it will be clearly
seen let me tell an old story. I have read in history that
two men were condemned to die as martyrs in the burning days of Queen Mary. One of them boasted loudly
to his companion of his confidence that he should play the
man at the stake. He did not mind the suffering, he was
so grounded in the Gospel that he knew he should never
deny it. He said that he longed for the fatal morning
even as a bride for the wedding.

His companion in prison in the same chamber was a
poor trembling soul, who could not and would not deny
his Master; but he told his companion that he was much
afraid of the fire. He said he had always been sensitive
of suffering, and he was in great dread that when he began
to burn the pain might cause him to deny the truth. He
besought his friend to pray for him, and he spent his
time in weeping over his weakness and crying to God
for strength.

The other continually rebuked him, and chided him
for being so unbelieving and weak. When they both
came to the stake, he who had been so bold recanted at
the sight of the fire and went back ignominiously to an
apostate's life, while the poor trembling man whose prayer
had been, "Lead me not into temptation," stood firm as a
rock, praising and magnifying God as he was burned to a
cinder.

Weakness is our strength: and our strength is weakness. Cry unto God that he try you not beyond your strength; and in the shrinking tenderness of your conscious weakness breathe out the prayer, "Lead us not into temptation." Then if He does lead you into the conflict, His Holy Spirit will strengthen you, and you will be brave as a lion, before the adversary. Though trembling and shrinking within yourself before the throne of God, you would confront the very devil and all the hosts of hell without one touch of fear. It may seem strange, but so the case is.

III. And now I conclude with the last head—*the lessons which this prayer teaches.*

The first lesson from the prayer, "Lead us not into temptation." is this: *Never boast your own strength.* Never say, "Oh, I shall never fall into such follies and sins. They may try me, but they will find more than a match in me." Let not him that puts on his harness boast as though he were putting it off. Never indulge one thought of congratulation as to self-strength. You have no power of your own, you are as weak as water. The devil has only to touch you in the right place and you will run according to his will. Only let a loose stone or two be moved and you will soon see that the feeble building of your own natural virtue will come down at a run. Never court temptation by boasting your own capacity.

The next thing is, *never desire trial.* Does anyone ever do that? Yes; I heard one say the other day that God had so prospered him for years that he was afraid he was not a child of God, for he found that God's children were chastised, and therefore he almost wished to be afflicted. Dear brother, do not wish for that: you will meet with trouble soon enough. If I were a little boy at home, I do not think I should say to my brother, because he had been whipped, "I am afraid I am not my father's child, and fear that he does not love me because I am not smarting under the rod. I wish he would whip me just to let me know his love." No, no child would ever be so stupid. We must not for any reason desire to be afflicted or tried, but must pray, "Lead us not into temptation."

The next thought is, *never go into temptation.* The man who prays "Lead us not into temptation," and then goes into it is a liar before God.

The last word is, if you pray God not to lead you into temptation, *do not lead others there.* Some seem to be singularly forgetful of the effect of their example, for they will do evil things in the presence of their children and those who look up to them. Now I pray you consider that by ill example you destroy others as well as yourself. Do nothing, my dear brother, of which you have need to be ashamed, or which you would not wish others to copy. Do the right at all times, and do not let Satan make a "cat's paw" of you to destroy the souls of others; do you pray, "Lead us not into temptation"? Then do not lead your children there. They are invited during the festive season to such and such a family party, where there will be everything but that which will conduce to their spiritual growth or even to their good morals; do not allow them to go. Put your foot down. Be steadfast about it. Having once prayed, "Lead us not into temptation," act not the hypocrite by allowing your children to go into it.

God bless these words to us. May they sink into our souls, and if any feel that they have sinned, oh that they may now ask forgiveness through the precious blood of Christ, and find it by faith in Him. When they have obtained mercy, let their next desire be that they may be kept in future from sinning as they did before, and therefore let them pray, "Lead us not into temptation."

CHAPTER ELEVEN

FIRST THINGS FIRST

A philosopher has remarked that if a man knew that he had thirty years of life before him, it would not be an unwise thing to spend twenty of those years in mapping out a plan of living, and putting himself under rule; for he would do more with the ten well-arranged years than with the whole thirty if he spent them at random. There is much truth in that saying. A man will do little by firing off his gun if he has not learned to take aim.

Possibly I address myself to some who have hitherto lived at haphazard; and if so, I invite them to a more hopeful method of living. To have a great many aims and objects is much the same thing as having no aim at all: for if a man shoots at many things he will hit none, or none worth the hitting. It is a grand thing to know what we are living for, and to live for a worthy object with the undivided energy of our being. Shall we, when the end comes, have made a success of life? Has our object been a right one, and has it been wisely pursued? Are the results of our conduct such as we shall wish them to have been when the conflict of this mortal life is over? These questions deserve consideration at once.

Another question arises out of them — *What position should religion occupy in reference to a man's life?* That is a question which naturally arises in the arranging of life; for, whatever we choose to think of it, there is such a thing as religion in the world, and there is within us some yearning after spiritual things. We cannot help feeling that we need somewhat more than this visible world can offer us. Many of us find our greatest joy in the cultivation of that feeling, for it is to us the token of our spiritual nature, and the prophecy of immortality. To us this life is mainly worth the living because it promises to be the introduction to a better life. Alas for life if this were all, and there were not a higher and better state of existence! No knell would be more doleful than that which signified the death of man's hope of immortality.

What position should religion occupy in your life and mine? The answer must depend very much upon another question—What is religion, and what does religion itself demand? What are the requirements of the great God, and of the soul, and of eternity? This question has suggested to me our text:

"Seek ye first the kingdom of God, and His righteous-ness; and all these things shall be added unto you."
—(Matthew 6:33)

Here is an account of what true religion is. According to the words of Christ Jesus our Lord, it is "the kingdom of God and His righteousness."

Fretful anxiety is forbidden to the Christian. In the first place it is *needless.* Matthew 6:26: "Behold the fowls of the air," said Christ: "they sow not, neither do they reap, nor gather into barns; yet your heavenly Father feedeth them. Are ye not much better than they?" If you have a Father in heaven to care for you, are you not put to shame by every little bird that sits upon the bough and sings, though it has not two grains of barley in all the world? God takes charge of the fowls of the air, and thus they live exempt from care; why do not we?

Our Lord also taught that such anxiety is *useless* as well as needless; for, with all our care, we cannot add a cubit to our stature. Can we do anything else by fretful care? What if the farmer deplores that there is no rain? Do his fears unstop the bottles of heaven? Or if the merchant sighs because the wind detains his laden ship, will his complainings turn the gale to another quarter? We do not better ourselves a bit by all our fret and fume. It were infinitely wiser to do our best, and then cast our care upon our God. Prudence is wisdom, for it adapts means to ends; but anxiety is folly, for it groans and worries, and accomplishes nothing.

Besides, according to our Saviour, anxiety about carnal things is *heathenism:* "After all these things do the Gentiles seek." They have no God and no providence, and therefore they try to be a providence to themselves. As for the man of God who can say, "God's providence is mine inheritance," why should he pine away with trouble? Let the heir of heaven act a nobler part than the mere man of the world, who has his portion in this life, and lives without God and without hope. Our distrust of our God is childish and dishonoring.

It is plain that within us there is a propensity to be anxious. Can we not utilize it? Can we not turn it to account? I think so. Some are naturally thoughtful and careful; can they not transform this tendency into a benefit? We have a tendency to be anxious. Very well, let us be anxious; but let our anxiety run in the right direction. Here is a mental heat; let us apply it to some useful purpose. Our text sets before us *the true sphere of Christian carefulness.* "Seek ye first the kingdom of God, and His righteousness." Seek *that* with all your care; seek *that* with all your energy. Be anxious about *that*. Let your whole mind run in *that* direction with eagerness and thought. You cannot be too careful or too energetic when God and righteousness are concerned.

In our text there is a description of true religion; what

is it? "The kingdom of God." Without using a single
superfluous theological term, I may say that the great
God has always had a kingdom in this world. In the
olden times He set up a kingdom among His people Israel,
to whom He gave laws and statutes; but now the Lord
is King over all the world: "The God of the whole earth
shall He be called." "The earth is the Lord's, and the
fulness thereof; the world, and they that dwell therein."
God has a kingdom in this world, but it is too much
neglected and forgotten of men. The first thing to be done
by us is to enter that kingdom. Blessed is that man who
has the Lord God to be his King, and has learned to
order his life according to divine law. The highest liberty
comes from wearing the yoke of God. The servant of
men who dares not call his soul his own is a serf to be
pitied; but the servant of God, who fears nothing but sin,
is a man of princely mould. We must stoop before God,
that we may conquer among men. If we determine to
yield ourselves wholly unto the Lord, we shall become
influential among our fellow-men.

We can only enter into this kingdom of God by being
born again of His Spirit; for "except a man be born again,
he cannot see the kingdom of God." In that new birth
we learn to submit ourselves to the Lord Jesus Christ,
and to find in Him eternal life. God has appointed the
Lord Jesus heir of all things; by Him also He made the
worlds. He says of Him, "Kiss the Son, lest He be angry,
and ye perish from the way, when His wrath is kindled
but a little." Faith in Christ casts our sins at the foot of
His Cross, and brings us an inward life unto holiness. We
must believe in Jesus, and trust in His great atonement for
sin, for apart from His full atonement there is no salvation, and no true service of God. This faith puts us into
the kingdom of God; for to "as many as received Him,
to them gave He power to become the sons of God, even

to them that believe on His name." The first anxiety of every man should be to be a loyal subject of the kingdom of God.

When we feel that we are reconciled to God, and are under His supreme sway, our next object should be to continue there, and to become more and more completely obedient to divine rule, so that we may more fully enjoy every privilege of the kingdom. In the kingdom of God every man is a king and a priest. He that serves God reigns. He that serves God is the possessor of all things. All things are ours when we are Christ's.

Our next business should be to spread that kingdom— to try to bring others under the dominion of Christ. It should be the lifework of each man to bring others to own the sovereignty of the Lord Jesus. What opportunities most of you possess! Your station, your education, your wealth, all give you advantages for serving the Lord. Are you using them? It is a great joy to the Christian minister to have about him a people who are missionaries in their daily lives.

This is the meaning of that first word—"Seek the kingdom of God." The reign of our Lord is to be our main object if we would lead a well-ordered, useful, happy and honored life.

Our text has a second word: "Seek first the kingdom of God *and His righteousness*," by which I understand the practical part of true religion. Seek to have the imputed righteousness of Christ by all means; but seek also to exhibit the infused righteousness which comes of sanctification. Brothers in Christ, let us aspire after a high degree of holiness. We are called to be saints; and saints are not miraculous beings to be set up in niches and admired; but they are men and women who live, and trade, and do righteousness, and practice charity in the streets of a city, or the fields of a village. Those who are

washed in the blood of the Lamb should not be satisfied
with the common cleanliness of morality; but the garment
of their life should be whiter than any fuller can make
it. Purity becomes the disciples of Jesus. In spirit, soul
and body we ought to be holiness to the Lord. Our righteousness must exceed that of the scribes and Pharisees:
it should be a reproduction of the character of our Lord.

True religion is diffusive and extensive in its opera-
tions. I see people drawing lines continually, and saying,
"So far is religious, and so far is secular." What do you
mean? The notion is one which suits with the exploded
notions of sacred places, priests, shrines and relics. I do
not believe in it. Everything is holy to a holy man. To
the pure all things are pure. To a man who seeks first
the kingdom of God and His righteousness, his house is
a temple, his meals are sacraments, his garments are vest-
ments, every day is a holy day, and he himself is a
priest and a king unto God. The sphere of Christianity
is co-extensive with daily life. I am not to say, "I serve
God when I stand in the pulpit"; for that might imply
that I wished to serve the devil when my sermon was
over. We are not only to be devout at church, and pious
at prayer-meetings; but to be devout and godly everywhere. Religion must not be like a fine piece of mediaeval
armor, to be hung upon the wall, or only worn on state
occasions. No; it is a garment for the house, the shop,
the bank. Your ledgers and safes are to be made by grace
"holiness unto the Lord." Godliness is for the parlor
and the drawing-room. It can neither be put off nor on.
It is of the man and in the man if it be real. Righteousness is a quality of the heart, and abides in the nature
of the saved man as a component part of his new self.
He is not righteous who is not always righteous.

I mentioned just now that true godliness must be diffusive, and I return to the statement. Hypocrites swallow

religion in lumps, inviting all to admire the quantity; but sincere seekers after righteousness quietly dissolve their godliness in their lives and sweeten all their common relationships therewith. The real saint flavors his ordinary life with grace, so that his wife, and his children, his servants and his neighbors, are the better for it. Mr. Rowland Hill used to say that a man was not a true Christian if his dog and his cat were not the better off for it. That witness is true. A man's religion ought to be to him what perfume is to a rose, or light to the sun; it should be the necessary outcome of his existence. If his life is not fragrant with truth, and bright with love, the question arises whether he knows the religion of our Lord Jesus. The division between sacred and secular is most unhappy to both divisions of life: we want them united again.

If we could only feel that our common acts are parts of a saintly life, they would not so often be done carelessly. If we lay our poor daily life by itself, it will be disregarded; but if we combine it with our holiest aspirations and exercises, it will be preserved. Our religion must be part and parcel of our daily life, and then the whole of our life will be preserved from the destroyer. Doth not the Scripture say, "Whether ye eat or drink, or whatsoever ye do, do all in the name of the Lord Jesus"?

"But," says one, "are we not to have amusements?" Yes, such amusements as you can take in the fear of God. Do whatever Jesus would have done. This is liberty enough for one who aspires to be like Jesus. There is happiness enough in things which are pure and right; and if not, we will not do evil to find more. We find pleasure enough without hunting for it in the purlieus of sin. There are joys which are as far above the pleasures of folly as the feasts of kings are above the husks of swine. At times our inner life flames up into a blaze of joy; and if usually it burns lower, there is at least a steady fire of peace upon our hearth which makes our life such that we envy none. It is not slavery that I set before you when I say that we are first of all to seek the kingdom of God and His righteousness: there is a present recompense which justifies the choice; and as for the eternal future, it pleads for it with voice of thunder.

Here is an account, also, of the proper position of true religion. "Seek ye *first* the kingdom of God and His righteousness."

Let the word "first" indicate to you the order of *time*. True godliness is as good for this life as for the next. If I had to die like a dog, I would still wish to be a Christian. Place religion first *in the order of time*. Begin each week by carefully consecrating the first day to rest and holy worship. Begin each day by giving the dew of the morning to communion with heaven. Begin your married life by seeking the blessing of the great Father, and choosing for a partner one that will agree with you in the fear of God. In opening a new business, sanctify the venture with the supplications of godly friends, and in all fresh enterprises be guided of the Lord. If we begin, continue and end with God, our way will be strewn with blessings.

Seek also the kingdom of God first *in order of preference*. If it should ever become a choice between God and Mammon, never hesitate. If wealth and righteousness run counter to each other, let the gold perish, but hold thou fast to righteousness. Follow Christ, however dear it cost thee. Blessed is that man who never deliberates, because his mind is made up rather to "suffer affliction with the people of God than to enjoy the pleasures of sin for a season." Blessed is the man who knows no policy but that of thorough consecration to God and righteousness— who is not careful to answer in this matter, but has his mind decided once for all.

"Well," cries one, "but, you know, we must live." I am

not sure about that. There are occasions when it would be better not to live. An old heraldic motto says, "Better death than false of faith." I am, however, quite clear about another necessity—*we must die;* and we had better take that "must" into consideration, and not quite so often repeat the cant phrase. "We must live."

Let godliness be first *in intensity.* It is to be feared that many give their force to their worldly pursuits, and their feebleness to their religion. They are "all there" during banking hours; but they are not "all there" at the hour of prayer. They remind me of one whose voice in our assemblies for prayer was exceedingly low, and well nigh inaudible; but in the shop he could be heard almost too well. Should it be so, that self should have our energies and Christ should have our lukewarmness? If ever we grow ardent and enthusiastic, it should be in the noblest of all causes, in the service of the best of Masters. In that work we cannot be too earnest; seldom enough do we meet with a person who verges upon excess of zeal in this matter. For Him who has redeemed us with His precious blood we cannot do too much; our heart complains that we cannot do enough. Alas! the comparative sizes of the Bible and the ledger are frequently symbolical: a neat little Bible is buried under a huge ledger. I claim for things divine a different place; let that be first which is first; throw your whole soul into the love and service of the Lord.

Seek the kingdom of God and His righteousness first, by giving to true religion *a sovereignty over your lives.* The helm by which life is steered should be in the hand of God. To glorify God and promote righteousness should be our master passion. This Aaron's rod should swallow up all other rods. Be first a man of God: after that a banker, or a merchant, or a working-man. I would to God that our politics, our merchandise, our literature, our

art, were all saturated with this idea—"First a Christian."
Then the secondary character would rise in excellence
and nobility. Science, social laws, trade usages, domestic
life, would all be the better for coming under the suprem-
acy of living religion. The fear of God should be the
foundation and the topstone of the social edifice. "Christ
first," and other things in their due order. Over and
above all, let consecration to God shine forth even as the
pillar of fire in the wilderness covered and illuminated
the entire camp of Israel.

Now to *the promise here made to those who "seek first
the kingdom of God, and His righteousness."* Does any
one demand, "What will become of our business if we place
godliness first?" The answer is in the text: "All these
things shall be added unto you." A young man beginning
life, resolving that he will do everything in the fear of
God, and that as God helps him he will do nothing that
is contrary to the mind of the Lord Jesus Christ—shall he
prosper? He shall get on so far as this: he shall have
bread to eat, and raiment to put on—all that is needful
for this life "shall be added to him."

"Alas!" sighs one, "I am out of place, and I know not
how to provide for myself and my household." Are you
sure that this trial has come without your own fault?
Then be not of doubtful mind, for the Lord will provide
for you. He has said, "Trust in the Lord and do good;
so shalt thou dwell in the land, and verily thou shalt be
fed." David's experience was, "I have been young and now
am old; yet have I not seen the righteous forsaken." The
drunken, the vicious, the idle, the dishonest may suffer
hunger, and it will be well for them if such discipline
amends them; but to the upright there arises light in the
darkness. They that serve God shall not have to complain
of His deserting them.

The blessings of this life come to gracious men in the

best shape and form; for they come by divine promise.
Suppose that it were now put into the power of each one
of us to be rich, I suspect that the most of us would be
eager to avail ourselves of the opportunity; and yet it is
a moot point whether it would be best for certain of us
to have the burden of wealth. It is a question whether
some people, who behave splendidly where they now are,
would be half as good, or a tithe as happy, if they were
lifted to higher positions. I have seen heroes drivel under
the influence of luxury. Many are the creatures of circumstances, and make but poor creatures when their circumstances allow of self-indulgence. We do not know
what is best for us. It is sometimes very much better for
us to suffer loss and disappointment than to obtain gain
and prosperity.

"All these things shall be added unto you," and the
measure of the addition shall be arranged by infallible
wisdom. Temporal things shall come to you in such proportion as you would yourself desire them, if you were
able to know all things, and to form a judgment according
to infinite wisdom. Would you not prefer a lot selected
by the Lord to one chosen by yourself? Do you not joy-
fully sing with the Psalmist, "Thou shalt choose mine
inheritance for me"?

Does not the promise also imply that needful things
shall come to the believer without vexatious worry and
consuming labor? While others are worrying, you shall be
singing. While others rise in the morning and cry, "How
shall we live through the day?" you shall wake to a secure
provision, and you shall have a happy enjoyment of it.
Your place of defense shall be the munitions of rocks;
your bread shall be given you, and your waters shall be
sure. Contentment with your lot, and confidence in God,
will make life peaceful and happy; a dinner of herbs with
content will yield a flavor of satisfaction unknown to

those who eat the stalled ox. It it better to be happy
than to be rich; and happiness lies in the heart rather
than in the purse. Not what a man has, but what a man
is, will decide his bliss or woe in this life and the next.
Oh yes, if God Himself adds to you the things of this
life, while you are serving Him, the lines will fall to you
in pleasant places, and you will have a goodly heritage.

This is what God intends to do in providence to the
man who serves Him heartily; He will add to him the
things of this life. These shall be thrown in as supplements to the divine heritage. I incur certain little outlays
in connection with my study; we need a few matters which
may be paid for out of petty cash; but I have never seen,
as far as I recollect, a single penny for string and brown
paper; because, as a reader and writer, I buy books, and
then the string and brown paper are added to me. My
purchase is the books, but the string and brown paper
come to me, added as a matter of course. This is the idea
of our text: you are to spend your strength on the high
and noble purpose of glorifying God, and then the minor
matters of what shall we eat? and what shall we drink?
and wherewithal shall we be clothed? are thrown in as
supplements. Earthly things are but the brown paper and
string; and I pray you never think too much of them.

Some people get so much of this brown paper and string
that they glory in them, and expect us to fall down and
worship them. If we refuse this homage, they are foolish
enough to adore themselves. It must not be so among
the servants of God. To us the man is the man, and not
the guinea's stamp. "All these things" are to us small
matters; the real life of the soul is all in all. Do not slice
pieces out of your manhood, and then hope to fill up the
vacancies with bank-notes. He who loses manliness or
godliness to gain gold is a great cheater of himself. Keep
yourselves entire for God and for His Christ, and let all

other matters be additions, not subtractions. Live above
the world. Its goods will come to you when you do not bid
high for them. If you hunt the butterfly of wealth too
eagerly you may spoil it by the stroke with which you
secure it. When earthly things are sought for as the main
object, they are degraded into rubbish, and the seeker
of them has fallen to be a mere man with a muck-rake,
turning over a dunghill to find nothing. Set your heart
on nobler things than pelf! Cry with David, "I will lift
up mine eyes to the hills whence cometh my help." Men
and brethren, let us so live that it will be safe for God
to add to us the blessings of the life that now is; but that
can only be done with safety when we have learned to
keep the world under our feet.

May the Lord enable us to live to high and noble pur-
poses, that so we may meet in the glory-land, and hear
the approving voice of Jesus, our Saviour and Captain,
saying to us, "Well done, good and faithful servants."

Chapter Twelve

"KNOCK"

"Ask, and it shall be given you; seek, and ye shall find; knock, and it shall be opened unto you."
— (Matthew 7:7).

In these three exhortations there would appear to be a gradation; it is the same thought put into another shape, and made more forcible. *Ask*—that is, in the quiet of your spirit, speak with God concerning your need, and humbly beg Him to grant your desires; this is a good and acceptable form of prayer. If, however, asking should not appear to succeed, the Lord would arouse you to a more concentrated and active longing; therefore let your desires call in the aid of knowledge, thought, consideration, meditation and practical action, and learn to *seek* for the blessings you desire as men seek for hidden treasures. These good things are laid up in store, and they are accessible to fervent minds. See how you can reach them. Add to asking the study of the promises of God, a diligent hearing of His word, a devout meditation upon the way of salvation, and all such means of grace as may bring you the blessing. Advance from asking into seeking. And if after all it should still seem that you have not obtained your desire, then *knock,* and so come to closer and more agonizing work; use not alone the voice, but the whole soul; exercise yourself unto godliness to obtain the boon; use every effort to win that which you seek after; for remember that doing is praying; living to God is a high

117

form of seeking, and the bent of the entire mind is knocking. God often gives to His people when they keep His commandments that which He denies to them if they walk carelessly. Remember the words of the Lord Jesus, how He said, "If ye abide in me, and My words abide in you, ye shall ask what ye will, and it shall be done unto you." Holiness is essential to power in prayer: the life must knock while the lips ask and the heart seeks.

I will change my line of exposition and say: ask as a *beggar* petitions for alms. They say that begging is a poor trade, but when you ply it well with God no other trade is so profitable. Men get more by asking than by working without prayer. Though I do not discommend working, yet I most highly commend praying. Nothing under heaven pays like prevailing prayer. He that has power in prayer has all things at his call. Ask as a poor mendicant who is hungry and pleads for bread. Then seek as a *merchant* who hunts for goodly pearls, looking up and down, anxious to give all that he has that he may win a matchless treasure. Seek as a *servant* carefully looking after his master's interests and laboring to promote them. Seek with all diligence, adding to the earnestness of the beggar the careful watchfulness of the jeweller who is seeking for a gem. Conclude all by knocking at mercy's door as a *lost traveler* caught out on a cold night in a blinding sleet knocks for shelter that he may not perish in the storm. When you have reached the gate of salvation ask to be admitted by the great love of God, then look well to see the way of entering, seeking to enter in; and if still the door seems shut against you, knock right heavily, and continue knocking till you are safely lodged within the home of love.

Once again, ask for what you want, seek for what you have lost, knock for that from which you are excluded.

Perhaps this last rearrangement best indicates the shades of meaning, and brings out the distinctions.

I. First, then, dear friend, whoever you are, if you are desirous of entering into eternal life, I would expound to you the inscription over the gate, by saying, first, *the door of mercy may appear to you to be closed against you.* That is implied in the text; "Knock, and it shall be opened unto you." If to your consciousness the door stood wide open, there would be no need of knocking; but since in your apprehension it is closed against you, it is for you to seek admission in the proper way by knocking.

To a large extent this apprehension is the result of your own fears. You think the gate is closed because you feel it ought to be so; you feel that if God dealt with you as you would deal with your fellow-men, He would be so offended with you as to shut the door of His favor once for all. You remember how guilty you have been, how often you have refused the divine call, and how you have gone on from evil to evil, and therefore you fear that the Master of the house has already risen up and shut to the door. You fear lest like the obstinate ones in Noah's day you will find the door of the ark closed, and yourself shut out to perish in the general destruction. Sin lieth at the door, and blocks it.

Let me, however, warn you that *the door can be closed and kept shut by unbelief.* He that believeth entereth into Christ when he believeth; he that cometh in by the door shall be saved, and shall go in and out and find pasture; so our Lord says in the tenth of John. "He that believeth in Him hath everlasting life," there is no question about that; but we read on the other hand, "So then they could not enter in because of unbelief." Forty years the tribes were in the wilderness, going toward Canaan, yet they never reached the promised land because of unbelief. And what if some of you should be forty years attending this means of grace? Coming and going, coming and going, hearing sermons, witnessing ordinances and joining with God's people in worship; what if after all the forty years you should never enter in because of unbelief? Souls, I tell you if you lived each one of you as long as Methuselah, you could never enter in unless you believed in Jesus Christ. The moment you have trusted Him with your whole heart and soul you are within the blessed portals of the Father's house, but however many years you may be asking, seeking and knocking, you will never enter in till faith comes, for unbelief keeps up the chain of the door, and there is no entering in while it rules your spirit.

II. Secondly, *a door implies an opening*. What is a door meant for if it is always to be kept shut? The wall might as well have remained without a break. It would be of no use to knock at a wall, but you may wisely knock at a door, for it is arranged for opening. You will enter in eventually if you knock on, for *the Gospel is good news for men*, and how could it be good news if it should so happen that they might sincerely come to Christ and ask mercy, and be denied it? I fear that the Gospel preached by certain divines sounds rather like bad news than good news to awakened souls, for it requires so much feeling and preparation on the sinner's part that they are not cheered nor led to hope thereby. But be sure that the Lord is willing to save all those who are willing to be saved in His own appointed way. God is satisfied with Christ, and if you are satisfied with Christ, God is satisfied with you. This is glad tidings to every soul that is willing to accept the atonement made, and the righteousness prepared by the Lord Jesus.

Dear friend, *this Gospel must be meant to be received by sinners,* or else it would not have been sent. "But," saith one, "I am such a sinner." Just so. You are the sort of person for whom the news of mercy is intended. A gospel is not needed by perfect men; sinless men need no pardon. No sacrifice is wanted if there is no guilt; no atonement is wanted where there is no transgression. They that are whole need not a physician, but they that are sick. This door of hope which God has prepared was meant to be an entrance into life, and it was meant to open for sinners, for if it does not open to sinners it will never open at all; for we have all sinned, and so we must all be shut out unless it be of free grace for those who are guilty.

III. Thirdly, knock, for *a knocker is provided.* What is this knocker? First of all, it may be found in *the promises of God.* We are sure to speed well when we can plead a promise. It is well to say unto the Lord, "Do as Thou hast said." What force abides in an appeal to the word, the oath, and the covenant of God. If you can only quote a promise applicable to your condition, and spread it before the Lord in faith, and say, "Remember this word unto Thy servant upon which Thou hast caused me to hope," you must obtain the blessing. Pleading the promise gives such a knock at the gate of heaven that it must be opened.

The great knocker, however, is *the name of the Lord Jesus Christ.* Now, when we go to God and plead the name of Christ, it means that we plead the authority of Christ, that we ask of God as though we were in Christ's stead, and expect Him to give it to us as if He were giving it to Jesus. That is something more than pleading for Christ's sake. I suppose the apostles at first did plead with God for Christ's sake, but Jesus says to them, "Hitherto ye have asked nothing *in My name.*" It is a higher grade of prayer, and when we get to pleading Christ's name with the Father, then do we gloriously prevail. Plead the precious blood of Jesus Christ, and you have knocked so that you must be heard.

"Alas!" says one, "I see the knocker, for I know something of the promises and of the person of our Lord, but how am I to knock?" With the hand of faith. Believe that God will keep His promise; ask Him to do so, and thus knock. Believe that Jesus is worthy, whose name you are pleading, and so knock in confidence that God will honor the name of His dear Son.

IV. Next, to you who are knocking at the gate *a promise is given*. That is more than having a door before you, or a knocker to knock with. The promise is above the gate in plain words. Read it. You are growing faint and weary; read the promise, and grow strong again. "Knock, and it shall be opened unto you." Observe how plain and positive it is with its glorious "shall" burning like a lamp in the center of it. In letters of love the inscription shines out amidst all the darkness that surrounds you, and these are its words, "It shall be opened unto you." If you knock at the door of the kindest of men you see no such promise set before you, and yet you knock, and knock confidently; how much more boldly should you come to the door of grace when it is expressly declared, "It shall be opened unto you"!

Remember that this promise was *freely given*. You never asked the Lord for such a word, it was uttered by spontaneous goodness. You did not come and plead with Jesus for a promise that you should be heard in prayer. Far from it—you did not even pray. Perhaps you have been living in the world forty years, and have never truly prayed at all; but the Lord out of His overflowing heart of generous love has made this promise to you, "Knock, and it shall be opened unto you." Wherefore do you doubt? Do you think He will not keep His word? A God who cannot lie, who was under no necessity to promise, freely, out of the greatness of His divine nature, which is love, says to a poor sinner, "Knock, and it shall be opened unto you." Oh, be sure of this, that He means it; and till heaven and earth shall pass away His word shall stand, and neither you nor any other sinner that knocks at His door shall be refused admittance.

The mercy is that *this promise is meant for all knockers* —"Knock, and it shall be opened unto *you*." The Lord has not denied to you the privilege of praying, or declared that He will not answer your requests. You may knock, and you may expect to see the door open. The Lord knows who will knock, for "the Lord knoweth them that are His." But knock, my friend, knock now, and it will soon be seen that you are one of God's chosen ones. It is a rule with the Lord that to him that knocketh it shall be opened.

Blessed be God, this text of mine shines out as if printed in stars, and *it continues to shine from day-dawn of life to set of sun.* As long as a man lives, if he knocks at God's door, it shall be opened unto him. You may have been long a rebel, and you may have heaped up your sins till they seem to shut out all hope from you, but still knock at Christ, the door, for an opening time will come. Even if it were with your expiring hand, if you could knock at mercy's gate it would open to thee; but put not off thy day of knocking because of God's long-suffering mercy. I will be bound for God as a hostage that He will answer you. I sought the Lord, and He heard me; and since then I have never doubted of any living soul but that if he too will seek the Lord through Jesus Christ he will certainly be saved. Oh, that you would try it! The Lord move you thereto by His own blessed Spirit. When, in answer to your knocking, you see the door move, then arise, and tarry not.

CHAPTER THIRTEEN

THE SIEVE

*"Not every one that saith unto me, Lord, Lord, shall
enter into the kingdom of heaven; but he that doeth
the will of my Father which is in heaven"*
                              —(Matthew 7:21).

In reading this chapter one is led to feel that it is not,
after all, an easy thing to be a sincere Christian. The way
is hard, the road is narrow. Who will may represent the
way to heaven as being easy; our Saviour does not so
speak of it. "Strait is the gate and narrow is the way,
and few there be that find it." "Many are called and few
chosen." The difficulty of being right is increased by the
fact that there are men in the world whose trade it is to
make counterfeits. There were, and there are, many false
prophets. Our Saviour has spoken about them in this
chapter, and given us a way of testing them; but they are
carrying on their trade still as successfully as ever. Now,
since there are traitors abroad whose business it is to
deceive, we ought to be doubly vigilant and constantly
upon our watch-tower, lest we be misled by them. I
charge you, examine every statement you hear from Christian pulpits and platforms; I charge you, sift and try every
religious book by the great standard of the Word of God.
Believe none of us if we speak contrary to this Word—
yea, believe not an angel from heaven if he preach any
other gospel than that which is contained in inspired
Scripture. "To the law and to the testimony, if they speak

THE SERMON ON THE MOUNT · 125

not according to this word it is because there is no truth in them." God grant us grace to escape from false prophets! We shall not do so if we are careless and off our guard, for the sheep-skin garment so effectively covers the wolf, the broad phylactery so decorates the hypocrite, that thousands are deceived by the outward appearance, and do not discover the cheat. Crafty are the wiles of the enemy, and many foolish ones are still ignorant of his devices. Tutored by the experience of ages, seducers and evil men not only wax worse and worse, but they grow more and more cunning. If it were possible, they would deceive even the very elect. Happy shall they be, who, being elect, are kept by the mighty power of God unto salvation, so that they are not carried away with any error.

In addition to the fact that there are false teachers, so is it certain that there are false professors. There never was a time in the church of God in which all were Christians who professed to be so. Surely the golden age of the church must have been when the Master Himself was in it, and had selected twelve choice spirits to be nearest to His person, and to act, as it were, the prime ministers of His kingdom; yet there was a devil amongst the twelve, a devil in the church of which Jesus was pastor. Judas, the treasurer of the apostles, was also a son of perdition. When Paul and the apostles kept watch over the elect church, surely that must have been a happy time; and when persecution raged all around, and acted like a great winnowing fan to drive away the chaff, one would have expected to find that the threshing-floor contained only clean grain; but it was not so, the heap upon the threshing-floor of the church was even then a mingled mass of corn and chaff. Some turned aside from love of the world, and others were deluded into grievous error, while there were others who remained in the church to discredit it by their impurity, and to bring chastisements upon it by their sin. We shall never see a perfect church till we see the Lord face to face in heaven.

Now, if in the church of God there are those who are deceivers and deceived, the question comes to each one of us, "May not we also be mistaken? Is it not possible that we, though making a profession of religion, may, after all, be insincere or deluded in that profession, and fail to be what we think we are?" Therefore let us put ourselves at this time into the attitude of self-examination, and whatever is spoken, let it come home to us personally. May we try ourselves whether we be right or no, not flinching from any pointed truth; but anxiously desiring to be tried and tested before the Lord Himself.

The text I would bring before you by noticing, first, that it contains *a commendable expression,* "Lord, Lord;" but, secondly, *it was used by gross hypocrites;* and then, thirdly, we shall show *wherein these hypocrites failed—* what it was that they lacked which rendered it impossible that they should enter into the kingdom.

I. First, then, the text contains *a commendable speech.* We may be sure the speech was a good one, or the hypocrites would not have used it as a cloak for their hypocrisy. Men do not use dubious expressions when they want to appear exceedingly devout. They take care, however bad their deeds may be, to make their words at any rate sound well. Therefore the persons spoken of in the text said to Jesus, "Lord, Lord." It is a fitting mode of speech for each one of us to use.

At first, dear friends, we ought to say to Jesus, "Lord, Lord," in reference to His divinity. How can we be saved if we do not? Jesus Christ of Nazareth is to us Lord and God. We do not hesitate to use the language of Thomas when he put his finger into the print of the nails, and to say to Him, "My Lord and my God." Let others say of

Him what they will, and make Him to be a mere man, or a prophet, or a delegated God, such talk is nothing to the point with us; we believe Him to be very God of very God, and worship Him this day as He is enthroned in the highest heavens, believing Him to be worthy of the adoration which is due to God alone. I do not wonder that those who believe our Lord Jesus Christ to be a mere man say severe things of us; nor must they wonder if we deliver ourselves of strong utterances with regard to them. If we are wrong, we are idolaters, for we worship a person who is only a man; if we are right, much of their teaching is blasphemous, for they deny the deity of the Christ of God. There is a great gulf between us, and it is only common honesty to admit it. To conceal the fact in order to be thought liberal would be a mean artifice, unworthy of an honest man. The question in debate is a vital one, and there can be no halting place between one view or the other. Compromise must always be impossible where the truth is essential and fundamental. There are some points in which we may agree to differ, but these are points in which there can be no mutual concessions or tonings down of statement. Christ Jesus is either God or He is not, and if He be God, as we believe He is, then those who reject His deity cannot be true believers in Him, and, therefore, must miss the benefits which He promises to those who receive Him. I cannot conceive any man to be right in religion if he be not right in reference to the person of the Redeemer. "You cannot be right in the rest unless you think rightly of Him." If you will not have Him to be your God, neither will He save you. Let His abundant miracles, His divine teaching, His unique character, and His resurrection convince you that "the Word was God," and is in all respects equally divine with the Father and the Spirit.

The expression before us is commendable under another

aspect, one in which likely it was used by these hypocrites.
We use it toward Christ to denote that we own Him to
be our Master; He is "Lord, Lord" to us. In the true
Church of Christ there are no lords but this one Lord.
"One is your Master, even Christ, and all ye are brethren."
As servants of one common Master, we stand upon an
equality. Did He not say, "The rulers of the Gentiles exercise lordship over them, but it shall not be so among
you." Christ is Lord to us, and none else in the church
of God. And the church takes care, when she is in a
right state, that there shall never be any legislator for her
except Christ. He is her law-maker, and not Parliaments
or kings. Doctrine comes from His lips and from His
word, but from no councils and no teachers or divines.
As to the rules of the church, if they are not the rules of
Jesus, given by the authority of His Spirit, they are no
rules for us. As for human traditions, prescriptions, and
ordinances in reference to religion, rend them to pieces and
toss them to the winds. Unto Jesus, who was once nailed
to the tree, be honor throughout all ages. He is Lord,
Lord, in that sense.

As He is thus beyond all controversy Lord divinely and
Lord as legislator, it is right that this should be spoken.
It was a brave thing for the Covenanters of Scotland to
be ready to die for the headship of Christ in His church,
and I trust there are thousands still alive who would as
gladly relinquish life itself to preserve the crown-right
of our exalted Lord. It would be well worth any man's
while to lay down his life to defend the deity of Christ,
which doctrine cannot be taken away without removing
the very foundations of the faith; and if the foundations
be moved, what can the righteous do? Bear your testimony, then, you followers of the Lamb, and be not afraid
to own His name. Though hypocrites have said it, you
need not blush to say it; for it is most true that Jesus is

both Lord and God. Say "Lord, Lord" with unfaltering
tongue. Say it daily by your actions. Have respect unto
your Master, and let others see that you respect Him.
Do *this* good action because Christ bids you; refuse to do
that evil thing because Christ forbids you. Move in *that*
line, because He leads the way; refuse that other line,
because you see not His footprints there. Let all men see
that you practically say, "Lord, Lord," whenever you
think of Jesus. This is the very spirit of Christianity—
to do what Christ bids us, and to honor Him in heart
and lip and life evermore. I wish that some Christians
were a little more outspoken in their acknowledgment
of their great Lord and Master; and I commend these
hypocrites, if I can commend them at all, that they wisely
choose a fit and godly speech, though, alas! they dishonored
the good speech, by using it so foully, when they said
"Lord, Lord."

II. And now, secondly, *there were hypocrites who used
this excellent mode of speech.* What sort of people were
they who said "Lord, Lord"? And yet the Master says of
them, that not every one of them shall enter into the
kingdom of heaven? Well, I think He refers to a considerable number of people, and I will seek them out. I wonder
whether I shall find any among you. Help me, my brethren,
by your own self-examination to discover these people.

There can be no doubt that our Lord referred, in the
first place, to a certain class of superficial externalists,
who said "Lord, Lord," and there their religion ended.
Such persons still exist all around us. They are superficial in nature, and in general character. They say good
things, but they never feel what they say. Their pious
expressions come from as low as the throat, but never
from the abysses of the heart. They are of the stony
ground order, and have no depth of earth; the hard, barren
rock is barely concealed by a sprinkling of soil. They

may accurately be styled externalists, for they have the
notion that when they have attended to the outside of
godliness the whole matter is fully discharged. For instance, if they sing with their voice, they conclude that
they have praised God, and that when the hymn is all
uttered to melodious notes worship has been presented
to God, even though the heart has never praised Him at
all. When they bow the head and close their eyes in
public prayer, they consider they are doing something
right and proper, though likely they are thinking of their
farm, their garden, their children, or their home, casting
up their accounts, and wondering how they will find trade
and the money-market on Monday when they get to their
shops. The externalists are satisfied with the shell of
religion whether life remains therein or no; they have a
form of godliness, but they are strangers to its power.

Another class of persons who say "Lord, Lord," and yet
are not saved are those who regard religion as a excellent
thing for quieting their conscience, but who do not look
upon it as a practical influence which is to affect their
lives and to influence their conduct. I have known persons
who certainly would not be easy if they had not gone
through their morning and evening prayers, and yet they
were bad husbands and quarrelsome neighbors. They could
falsify an account, and put down an article twice to a
customer without a great disturbance of their self-satis-
faction, but they would not like to have been away from
the house of God on Sunday, or to have heard an unsound
discourse. Either of these things would have touched
their conscience, though it was callous on the point of
unfair dealing. They could lie, could lie handsomely,
but they would not swear, or sing a song; they drew the
line somewhere, and compounded for a thousand sins of
dishonesty by avoiding certain other vices; thus being

left to cheat themselves as a righteous punishment for cheating others.

Oh, the deceits and cheats which men play upon themselves! they are their own most easy dupes. A mere matter of religious form will outweigh the most important matters of virtue, when the judgment is perverted by folly. Their eye sees motes and overlooks beams, their judgment strains as gnats and flies, and yet it swallows camels and elephants. They leap one hour and limp another. They are minute on points of ritual, and equally lax as to common honesty; the thing really worth having— love to God, and love to man—they fling behind their backs, and fancy they shall be saved because they have complimented God by a hypocritical pretence of worship, and have deceived men by sanctimonious pretensions. As though, if I cheated a man every day I could make up for it by taking my hat off in the streets to him. They bow to the Almighty and rebel against Him. Do they fancy He is to be cozened by them? Do they dream that He is gratified by their sounding words and empty declarations? Whatever they may imagine, it is not so. Many say "Lord, Lord," to quiet their conscience, but enter the kingdom of heaven they never can.

We have also met with others who say, "Lord, Lord," but not in sincerity. They are busy professors, always ready to do anything, and they are not happy unless they have something to do. I blame them not for being busy: I would to God that the sincere people were half as busy; but I detect in them this vice: they are fondest of doing that which will be most seen; they prefer to serve God in those places where the most honor will be gained. To speak in public is infinitely preferable to them to the visitation of a poor sick woman. To work or to give where the deed will be blazoned abroad is after their minds. To take the chair at a public meeting, and receive a vote of

thanks, is delightful to them; but to go into a back street
and look after the poor, or plod on in Sunday school in
some inferior class, is not according to their taste. It
may seem harsh, but it is nevertheless true that many
are serving themselves under the pretence of serving
Christ; they labor to advance the cause in order that they
may be themselves advanced; and they push themselves
forward in the church this way and that way for the
glory of place and position, that everyone may say, "What
a good man that is, and how much influence he has, and
how well he serves his Master!" Beloved, if you and I
do anything nominally for God, and at the bottom we are
doing it for the sake of praise, it is not for God; we are
doing it for ourselves. I would like your conscience to
ask you, as my conscience is asking me, "Do I really serve
the Lord, or do I work in the church in order that I may
be consdered to be an industrious, praiseworthy minister,
seeking the good of my fellow-men?" I charge you before
God, shun the desire of human praise and never let it
pollute your motives. May the Holy Ghost purify you
from so base a motive. The praise of God—to have it said
by Him, "Well done, good and faithful servant"—*that* you
should seek; but honor from men, avoid it as you would a
viper. Shake it off into the fire, if ever you find the desire
of it clinging to your soul, else it may be your unhappy
lot to find at last that saying, "Lord, Lord," will not
secure you an entrance into the kingdom.

In all churches I fear there are some of another class
of hypocrites who say "Lord, Lord," for the sake of what
they can get by it. They believe that if gain is not godliness, godliness may be made helpful to gain. These gen-
tlemen flourish in all quarters of town and country. One
of them set up in a village, and the first question he
asked before he opened his shop was, "Which is the most
respectable congregation in the neighborhood," his object

being to go there, that he might not only get good, but dispose of his goods as well. We meet with persons in another rank in life whose object in attending a place is that they may get into a respectable circle, and have wealthy friends, and have their hand upon the door-handle of society. Swimming with the stream is their delight, and they prefer that stream in which there are the most gold fish.

Well, the list is sorrowfully long, but I must mention one or two others. One is the Sunday Christian. I dare say he is here now. He is an excellent Christian on the Lord's Day. As soon as the sun shines upon the earth on the first day of the week, all his religion is awake, but, alas, he is a very queer Christian on a Monday, and a remarkably bad Christian on Saturday nights. Many people keep their piety folded up and put away with their best clothes, and they only give it an airing on Sunday. Their Bible is to be seen under their arm on Sunday, but on Monday, where is that Bible? Well, not at the man's right hand, as a perpetual companion. Where are the precepts of Scripture? Are they in the shop? Are they in the house? Alas, the golden rule has been left in church to lie dusty in the pews until next Sunday. Religion is not wanted by some people on a week-day, it might be inconvenient. Many there be who sing psalms of praise to God but confine their praises to the congregation; as to praising Him in their heart at home, it never occurs to them. Their whole religion lies inside the meeting-house walls, or comes up at certain times and seasons during the day, when the family is called in to prayer. May God save us from intermittent religion! May He grant us grace to be always what we should wish to be if we were about to die. May religion never be to us a coat or a cloak to be taken off, but may it be intermingled with the warp and woof of our nature, so that we do not so much

talk religion as breathe and live it. I desire to eat and
drink and sleep eternal life, as an old divine used to say.
May that be ours. Good John Newton used to say of his
Calvinism, that he did not preach it in masses of dry
doctrine like pieces of lump sugar, but that it was stirred
up in all his preaching, like sugar dissolved in our tea.
Oh, that some of those people who keep lumps of religion
for Sundays would sweeten their lives and tempers with
it, till men could see that their ordinary every-day actions
were full of the grace of God, and that they were actu-
ated at all times by the love of the Most High. God save
us from being Sunday Christians.

III. *Where did these people fail?* That is the last point.
The Saviour said that they did not His sayings. "He that
doeth the will of my Father which is in heaven," says
He, "shall enter the kingdom." What is the will, then, of
His Father in heaven? We are expressly told that this is
the will of Him that sent Christ, that whosoever seeth
the Son and believeth on Him should not perish. It is a
part, then, of the will of God, which we must do if we
would be saved, that we believe on Jesus Christ. Hast
thou believed in Jesus? If not, thy sacraments, thy church-
goings, thy chapel-goings, thy prayers and hymns, all go
for nothing. If you do not trust in Jesus, you have not even
the foundation stone of salvation; you are lost; and may
God have mercy upon you!

It is a part of God's will, moreover, that where there
is faith there should be obedience to God, conformity to
the divine precepts. In fact, true faith in Jesus always
brings this. There never was a man that believed in Jesus
yet but what he sought to do the will of Jesus. Now it is
a part of the will of Jesus that all those who are His
should love one another. Hypocrites do not love one another; though they are always talking about the want of
love there is in the church. Listen to them! They are

always denouncing other people, and this is no mark of love to the brethren. They have a keen eye for the imperfections of others, but they have no love to those they censure. We must love the brethren, or we lack the plainest and most needful evidence of salvation, "for we know that we have passed from death unto life, because we love the brethren."

The true child of God, also, adds to his faith, love, and faith begets in him all the graces and virtues which adorn renewed manhood and bring glory to God. Alas! I have known some high professors, not commonly truthful, who would talk about communion with Christ and sweet enjoyments of divine love, and yet they seemed to miscalculate the multiplication table, and did not know how many pounds went to a hundred-weight. How swells the love of God in a man who is a thief? How can it be that he is a servant of a just and holy God, when he is unjust in his dealings toward his fellow-men? It will not do, sir. You may prate as long as you will, but you are no Christian unless the rule of integrity is the rule of your life.

Ay, and there are some who are unchaste, and yet dare to talk about being Christians. There are some who make a church their place of pretended worship, and profess to hear the words spoken with pleasure, who are a disgrace to Christianity all the time. Let them get home to their knees and pray God to give them manliness enough at least to be damned honestly, and not to go down to perdition wearing the name of Christian when Christians they are not. If I served Satan, and loved the pleasures of sin, I would do so out-and-out like a man; but to sneak into the church of God, and to live unchastely—I have no words sufficiently strong with which to denounce such detestable meanness.

Alas, I must add that there are some professed Christians who are not sober. If a man is not temperate in meats and drinks how dare he talk about the power of prayer? How dare he come to the prayer-meeting and open his mouth there? Do you suppose that Christ has any communion with Bacchus, that He will strike hands across the ale house bar, and call him a friend who staggers out of the door of the gin palace to go and listen to a sermon? "Is that ever done?" says one. Done? Many must confess that they have done it time and again! How dare they say, "Lord, Lord," and yet drain the drunkard's bowl in secret? O sirs, I don't want to put any of these cases in such a way that you should be vexed and angry, and say, "He is personal"; but if you did say so I should not apologize, but should tell you that so long as you are personal in your offence to Christ I shall be personal in my rebukes. If you are personally insulting to the Saviour, you must expect the Saviour's servant to be personal in upbraiding you.

Once more, I fear there are in these days a large number of professors who never exercise real private prayer. The Saviour says He will say to them, "I never knew you"; now He would have known them if they had been accustomed to converse with Him in private prayer. Had they communed with Him in earnest supplications, the Lord Jesus could not then have said, "I never knew you," for they would each one have replied, "Not know me, Lord! I have wept before Thee in secret, when no other eye saw me but Thine. I brought Thee habitually my daily cares, and cast my burden upon Thee. Dost not Thou know me? I have spoken to Thee face to face, as a man speaketh with his friend. I know *Thee*, O my Lord, by joyous experience of Thy goodness, and therefore I am sure Thou knowest me. Thine answers to my prayers and Thy gifts of grace have been so constant that I am sure Thou knowest me. Who is there on earth Thou dost know if Thou dost not know me? Happy is the man who can speak thus; but alas, many are quite unable to make such a reply. I fear there are some professors who do not pray. You were baptized, and yet you do not pray. You have joined the church, and yet you restrain prayer. You dare come to the communion table, although for a long time you have lived without prayer, for I cannot call *that* prayer which you slobber over in the way you do with your morning prayer when you are in a hurry, and your evening prayer, when you are almost asleep. God bless you, beloved, and save you from sham praying and make you to have truth in your inward parts, and cause you to be sincere before the living God.

Now, I know what will happen. Some dear trembling heart will say, "I always thought I was a hypocrite; now I know I am. I have always been fretting and troubling about that." It generally falls out contrary to our desire, those who are not hypocrites think they are, while real hypocrites throw off our warnings as an ironclad man-of-war casts off the shots of an ordinary gun. I try to make caps to fit heads which deserve to be covered, but the people whose heads they will fit never put them on; and others for whom they were never intended at all—dear, loving, tender-hearted believers, always watchful and careful—are the very ones who will put them on their own heads, and cry "Yes, I fear I am the hypocrite." Ah, dear soul, do not write bitter things against yourself, because, if you will consider the matter, you will soon see that you are no hypocrite. Would you do anything to grieve Christ? Do you not, above all things, desire to trust Him? Do you know anyone to trust in but Jesus? Are you not depending upon Him? And though you could not say you would die for Him, yet I believe, if it came to the point, that your trembling faith would still keep alive, when that of some of the boastful ones, who, in their own esteem, are almost perfect, would give way, and end in apostasy.

To each one I would say, if you believe in the Lord Jesus Christ with all your heart, you are no hypocrite; and if any one of you has been a hypocrite, and has to plead guilty to many things I have mentioned, come to the foot of the Cross and say, "Jesus, Master, I the chief of sinners am, have mercy upon me now. Look on me, and let my sins pass away. Look on me, and let all cunning, and hypocrisy be driven far from me. Give me a new heart and a right spirit, and from this day make me Thy child, and I will glorify Thee, both on earth and in heaven, for ever and ever."

CHAPTER FOURTEEN

THE TWO BUILDERS AND THEIR HOUSES

"Therefore whosoever heareth these sayings of mine, and doeth them, I will liken him unto a wise man, which built his house upon a rock: and the rain descended, and the floods came, and the winds blew, and beat upon that house; and it fell not: for it was founded upon a rock. And every one that heareth these sayings of mine, and doeth them not, shall be likened unto a foolish man, which built his house upon the sand: and the rain descended, and the floods came, and the winds blew, and beat upon that house; and it fell: and great was the fall of it"—(Matthew 7:24-27).

I. We shall now proceed to the Master's parable, and will you please notice, first of all, *the two builders?*

The wise man and the foolish man were both engaged in precisely the same avocations, and to a considerable extent achieved the same design; both of them undertook to build houses, both of them persevered in building, both of of them finished their houses. The likeness between them is considerable.

They were equally impressed with the need of building a house. They perceived the necessity of shelter from the heavy rains, they were alike desirous of being shielded from the floods, and screened from the wind. The advantage of a house to dwell in was evident to both. Even, thus, at this period, there are many who are impressed with the conviction that they need a Saviour. You now admit that you must be forgiven, justified, regenerated and sanctified, and your desires are fervent; for all of which I am deeply grateful, but also deeply anxious. You are in crowds desirous of becoming builders, and although some are wise and some foolish, up to this present we can see no difference in you; for you seem to be equally convinced that you need eternal life, and a good hope for the world to come.

Nor does the likeness end here, for the two builders were both alike *resolved to obtain what they needed*—a house; and their determination was not in words only, but in deeds, for they both resolutely set to work to build. In the same way there are among us many who are resolved that if Christ is to be had, they will have Him; and if there is such a thing as salvation, they will find it. They are earnest, intensely earnest, and though some of them will fail, and some of them succeed, yet up to this point they are both alike, and none but He who searcheth all hearts can discern the slightest difference. I look with sadness upon the two pilgrims, with their faces zealously turned Zionward, and I sigh as I wonder which one will find the Celestial City, and which will join with Formalist and Hypocrisy, and perish on the Dark Mountains. We are glad to hear of yearning hearts and resolute determinations, but, alas! all is not wheat that grows in cornfields, all is not gold that glitters. Appearances are hopeful, but appearances are often deceptive. There may be a deep sense of need, and there may be a determined resolution to get that need supplied, and yet out of two seekers, one may find and the other may miss, one may be foolish and the other may be wise.

These two builders seem to have been *equally well skilled in architecture*. The one could build a house without receiving any more instruction than the other. I do not find that there was halt or pause on the part of either

because he could not turn an arch, or fix a truss. Evidently
they were both skilled workmen, well acquainted with
their art. So is it with many others. They know as far
as the theory goes what the plan of salvation is, as well
as I do. Yet, where the knowledge is the same, the ulti-
mate result may vary; two men may be equally well
instructed in the Scriptures, yet one of them may be wise
and the other foolish. To know what faith is, what repentance is, what a good hope in Christ is, may all be
yours, and yet it may but increase your misery for ever.
If ye know these things, happy are ye if ye do them.
It is not the hearer, but the doer of the word, that is
blessed.

Once more, *these two builders both persevered and finished their structure.* The foolish man did not begin to
build, and then cease his work because he was not able
to finish; but, as far as I know, his house was finished
with as much completeness as the other; and, perhaps,
furnished quite as well. If you had looked at the two
structures, they would have seemed equally complete
from basement to roof, and yet there was a great difference between them in a most essential point. Even thus,
alas! many persevere in seeking salvation until they
imagine that they have found it; they abide for years
in the full belief that they are saved; they cry, "Peace,
peace," and write themselves down among the blessed, and
yet a fatal error lies at the base of all their religion; all
their hopes are vain, and their life-work will prove to
be a terrible failure. The builders are much alike up to
this point, but yet in reality they are wide as the poles
asunder both in work and character. The one builder
is wise, the other foolish; the one superficial, the other
substantial; the one pretentious, the other sincere. The
wise man's work was honest work where men's eyes could
not judge of it, the other's work was only well wrought

above ground, there was nothing of reality in the hidden parts; and hence in due time the first builder rejoiced as he saw his house outlive the storm: the other with his house was swept away to total destruction.

II. Thus much upon the two builders, let us now think upon *their two houses.*

One chief apparent difference between the two edifices probably was this, *that one of them built his house more quickly than the other.* The wise man had to spend a deal of time in underground work. Luke tells us that he digged deep, and laid his foundation on a rock. Now that rock-blasting, that carving and cutting of the hard granite, must have consumed days and weeks. The foolish builder had not this delay to encounter; the sand was all smooth and ready for him; he was able to commence at once to lay his courses of brick, and raise the walls with all rapidity. But all haste is not good speed, and there be some who travel too fast to hold. Unsound professors are often very rapid in their supposed spiritual growth. They were yesterday unconverted, to-day they become believers, to-morrow they begin to teach, the next day they are made perfect. They appear to be born of full stature, and equipped at all points, like Minerva, when, according to the fable, she leaped from the brain of Jupiter. They come up in a night, and alas! too often, like Jonah's gourd, they perish also in a night.

Now I raise not a question concerning the genuine character of sudden conversions. I believe that sudden conversions are among the best and truest forms of conversion. Take, for instance, that of the Apostle Paul. But still there are among those who profess to have been suddenly converted a sadly numerous company who answer to the description I have just given, for they build quickly, much too quickly for the masonry to be well constructed and lasting.

Of the two houses, one was built, I doubt not, *with far less trouble than the other*. Digging foundations in hard rocks, as I have said, takes time, but it also involves labor. Oftentimes did that wise builder pause to wipe the sweat from his brow; oftentimes did he retire to his bed worn out with his day's work, and yet there was not a stone appearing above the soil. His neighbor, opposite, had run up the walls, had reached the gable, was almost about to put on the roof, before there was scarce a foot above the ground of the wise builder's structure. "Ah," said he of the sandy foundation, "your toil is needless, and you have nothing to show for it. See how quickly my walls have risen, and yet I don't slave as you do. I take things easily; I neither bore myself nor the rocks, and yet see how my house springs up, and how neat it looks! Your old-fashioned ways are absurd. You dig and hammer away down below there as if you meant to pierce the centre. Why not use your common sense, and go ahead as I do? Away with your sighing and groaning, do as I do, and rejoice at once. Anxiety will kill you." After this fashion are truly awakened souls, like "lamps despised of those who are at ease." One man jumps, as it were, into peace, and boasts himself secure; whether he is correct or not in his confidence, he does not pause to question, he is too comfortable to have time to inquire into that matter. The estate is fair, why worry about the title-deeds? The feast is rich, why tarry for the wedding-garments? If a doubt should arise, the carnally secure man ascribes it to Satan, and puts it aside, whereas it is his own conscience and the warning voice of heaven which bid him take heed and be not deceived. The prayer for the Lord to search and try his heart and his reins, he never sincerely offers. Such a man does not like self-examination, and cannot endure to be told that there must be fruits meet for repentance. He takes things at guesswork, comes to rash conclusions, and shuts his eyes to disagreeable facts. He dreams that he is rich and increased in goods, whereas he is naked, and poor and miserable. Alas, what a waking will be his!

His more serious companion aroused at the same time is, on the other hand, far more diffident and self-distrustful; when he prays his heart groans before God, yet he fears he does not pray aright, and never rises from his knees contented with himself. He is not quite so soon satisfied about the reality of his faith as the other; "Perhaps," says he, "after all it is not the faith of God's elect." He examines himself whether he be in the faith. He trembles lest he should have the form of godliness without the power. He is afraid of shams and counterfeits, and is for buying gold tried in the fire. "My repentance," saith he, "am I sure it is a real loathing of sin as sin, or did I only shed a tear or two under the excitement of a revival service? Am I sure that my nature is renewed by the work of the Holy Ghost, or is it mere reformation?" You see this second man has much exercise of soul, he labors to enter into rest, lest by any means he should seem to come short of it. He has many strivings, many anxieties, many searchings of heart, because he is sincere and fears to be deceived. From him the kingdom of heaven suffereth violence, he finds the gate strait and the way narrow, and that the righteous scarcely are saved.

Be thankful if you are among this second class, for these are the true sons of God, and heirs of immortality. Your house costs you more to build, but it will be worth the cost. O beware of wearing the sheep's clothing without the sheep's nature; beware of saying "Lord, Lord," while you are the servant of sin. Beware of getting up fictitious religion, borrowing your experience from biographies, picking up godliness at second-hand from your mothers and fathers, and friends and acquaintances.

Whatever it may cost you of heart-breaking and agony, see to it that the sure foundation is reached, and the house so builded, that it will endure the trials which will inevitably test it.

The higher the foolish man built the harder work he had to keep it upright, for of course every tier of bricks that he laid made the weight the greater, and caused the sand to give way. The nearer heaven the builder went the sooner his wall bowed to its fall. A man who only makes it his aim to be thought a respectable man by attending a place of worship, may manage pretty well to keep up such a low wall even without a foundation; another man who joins a worldly church—a church that makes no pretence of purity—can also succeed with ease; but if he joins a church of Jesus Christ which carefully seeks to preserve purity in its membership, he has hard work to live up to the standard required of him. Suppose, yet further, that he should become a deacon or an elder, and he is devoid of grace, his higher aim will cost him more by far—for there are more to look at him, and there is more required of him. Now he prays in public, now he speaks a word of instruction to inquirers, and what straits and shifts the poor man is driven to, how constantly out of his own mouth is he condemned? "Why," saith he in his heart, "I know nothing about these things in my soul, and yet I have to speak and act as if I were taught of God." The more spirituality you aim at, and the more usefulness you strive for, the worse for you, unless you have a good foundation to begin with, in true sincerity and real faith. So bad is the course of unsound religion, the further you go in it the worse it becomes.

The main difference, however, between the two houses did not lay in these cracks and settlements, nor in the cheapness or rapidity of the building—*it lay out of sight, underground.* It was all a matter of foundation. How many there are who suppose that if a thing is out of sight it may as well be out of mind! Who do you think is likely to dig down and see what the foundations are? "Well," says one, "I see no need for being over precise; I do not believe in being so particular. What nobody sees cannot signify."

That is how the foolish builder comforted himself, and he doubtless sneered at the wise builder as a poor miserable creature, who was righteous overmuch, and melancholy. Outward appearance is everything with men, but nothing with God. The essential difference between the true child of God and the mere professor is not readily to be discovered, even by spiritual minds; but the Lord sees it. It is a secret mysterious something which the Lord prizes, "for He knoweth them that are His." He separates between the precious and the vile. He putteth away the pretenders as dross, but he suffereth no sincere heart to be destroyed.

What, then, is this important matter? I answer it is just this. If thou wouldst be built on a rock, see to it that thou hast *a true sense of sin*. I do not say that a sense of sin is a preparation for Christ, and that we ought to put men back from the gospel till they feel their sin; but I do believe that wherever there is true faith in Jesus there goes with it a deep abhorrence of sin. Faith without contrition is a dead and worthless faith. When I meet with professors who talk lightly of sin, I feel sure that they have built without a foundation. If they had ever felt the Spirit's wounding and killing sword of conviction, they would flee from sin as from a lion or a bear. Truly forgiven sinners dread the appearance of evil as burned-children dread the fire. Superficial repentance always leads to careless living. Faith that was never bedewed with repentance never brings forth the flowers of holiness. Pray earnestly for a broken heart. Remember it is the contrite spirit that pleases God. Do not believe that you can have ground for rejoicing if you never saw reason for lamenting. The promised comfort is only secured to those who have been mourners (Matthew 5:4).

Next to this seek for *real faith*. Many things which men call faith are not the precious faith of God's elect. Sincere trust in Jesus Christ is counterfeited in a thousand ways, and often imitated so accurately that only by rigid self-examination shall you discover the cheat. You must lie flat upon Christ, the Rock; you must depend entirely upon Him, all your hope and all your trust must be in Him. If you believe with the heart, and not nominally, you are safe, but not otherwise. You must have true repentance and real faith, or you are foolish builders.

Furthermore, seek an *inwrought experience of divine truth*. Ask to have it burned into you. I tremble for our churches now that false doctrine is rife, because I fear that many are not established in the truth. I pray the Lord for you, my dear flock, that you may know the truth by being taught of the Lord, for then you will not be led aside. The thieves and robbers will come, but as Christ's sheep you will not hear them. It is one thing to have a creed; it is quite another thing to have the truth graven upon the tables of the heart. Many fail here because truth was never experimentally made their own.

Pray, moreover, that your *faith may produce personal holiness*. Do not believe yourself to be saved from sin while you are living in sin. If you can find pleasure in the lusts of the flesh, you are no child of God. If you are given to drunkenness—and, mark you, many professors are so, only they drink at home and are not seen in the streets—how dwelleth the grace of God in you? If you delight in idle songs, and frequenting places of vain amusement, you need not be long in weighing yourself, you are found wanting already. If you were renewed in the spirit of your mind, you would no more love these things than an angel would. There must be a newborn nature implanted, and where there is not this exemplified in holiness of life, you may build ever so high and prate ever so loudly about your building, it is a poor miserable shanty after all, and will fall in the last hurricane.

Want of depth, want of sincerity, want of reality in religion—this is the want of our times. Want of an eye to God in religion, lack of sincere dealing with one's own soul, neglect of using the lancet with our hearts, neglect of the search warrant which God gives out against sin, carelessness concerning living upon Christ; much reading about Him, much talking about Him, but too little feeding upon His flesh, and drinking of His blood—these are the causes of tottering professions and baseless hopes.

Thus have I tried to open up the parable: and I have not designed to discourage any sincere soul, my aim has been to say to you, "Make your calling and election sure. Build on Christ's love, sincerity, desire, the work of the Holy Spirit, and be not deceived."

III. So now I come, in the third place, to notice *the common trial of the two houses.*

Whether your religion be true or not, it will be tried; whether it be chaff or wheat, the fan of the Great Winnower will surely be brought into operation upon all that lies on the threshing-floor. If you have dealings with God, you have to do with a "consuming fire." Whether you be really or nominally a Christian, if you come near to Christ He will try you as silver is tried. Judgment must begin at the house of God, and if you dare to come in to the house of God, judgment will begin with you.

By the way, let us note that, if there are such trials for those who profess to be Christians, what will become of you who make no profession? If the righteous scarcely

be saved, where will the ungodly and the wicked appear?
If judgment begin with the house of God what will the
end be of them that believe not? Terrible thought! But
to return.

Trials will come to profession, whether it be true or
false. If I do not mistake the reference in the text to
rain, flood, wind, these trials will be of three sorts at
least. The rain typifies *afflictions from heaven*. God will
send you adversities like showers, tribulations as many
as the drops of the dew. Between now and heaven, O
professor, you will feel the pelting storm. Like other
men, your body will be sick; or if not, you shall have
trouble in your house; children and friends will die, or
riches will take to themselves wings, and fly like an eagle
towards heaven. You must have trials from God's hand;
and, if you are not relying on Christ, you will not be
able to bear them. If you are not, by real faith, one with
Jesus Christ, even God's rain will be too much for you.

But there will also arise *trials from earth*—"the floods
came." In former days the floods of persecution were more
terrible than now, but persecution is still felt; and if you
are a professor, you will have to bear a measure of it.
Cruel mockings are still used against the people of God.
The world no more loves the true church today than it
did in the olden times. Can you bear slander and reproach
for Jesus? Not unless you are firmly rooted and grounded.
In the day of temptation and persecution the rootless
plants of the stony ground are withered away.

Then there will come *mysterious trials* typified by "the
winds." The prince of the power of the air will assail
you, with blasphemous suggestions, horrible temptations,
or artful insinuations. He knows how to cast clouds of
despondency over the human spirit; He can attack the
four corners of the house at once by his mysterious agency;
he can tempt us in divers ways at the same time, and

drive us to our wits' end. Woe to thee, then, unless thou hast something to hold by better than the mere sand of profession!

Where there is a good foundation trials will do no hurt, but where there is no foundation they will frequently bring the man's profession down in ruin, even in this life. How many lose their religion at the very outset! Pliable and Christian both set out for the Celestial City, both aspiring to the crown of gold; but they fell into the Slough of Despond, and then, as one of them struggled out on the side nearest his own house, and went back to the City of Destruction, while the other strove manfully to reach the further shore, the difference between the wise and foolish pilgrim was made manifest.

After Christians have proceeded further they will be tried in other ways. Infidelities often try Christians, I mean doubts about the essentials of the faith, and all its doctrines; and those that are not well cemented to the rock are easily moved to unbelief. This is the age of infidelities, but they who are on the rock by a truthful experience are not moved.

Where the heart is really grounded upon the truth, you will find that heresies, as well as infidelities, have but little effect. The sound Christian is like a stone, if he is thrown into the pool of false doctrine, he may be wetted by it, but he does not receive it into his inner self, whereas the unsound professor is like a sponge, he sucks it all in greedily, and retains what he absorbs.

How many there are who are tried by worldliness, and if their religion be but mere profession, worldliness soon eats the heart of it as doth a canker, and they become even as others! If, however, the Christian man's heart is right with God, he comes out and is separate, and the pride of life does not entrap him.

IV. To close. Having thus mentioned the common trials

and the effects produced in this life, let me now remind
you of the *different results of the trials* in reference to
the life to come.

In the one case, the rain descended heavily, and threat-
ened to wash the house away, but it was built on a rock,
and not only did the house stand, but the man inside
found great comfort in it. He could hear the pelting tor-
rent beating on the roof, and sit and sing; when the gusts
came against the windows he would only be more happy
to think he had such a shelter. Then came the floods.
They would, if they could, have sapped and undermined
the foundations, but they took no effect on the granite
rock, and though the wind howled round the habitation,
every stone was well cemented, and all bound as with iron
bands to the grand old rock, and therefore the man was
safe and happy within, and above all, grateful that he
had built on such a foundation.

The Christian rests peacefully upon Christ. Troubles
come one after another, but they do not sweep him away,
they only endear to him the hope which is based upon
Christ Jesus. And when at last death comes, that awful
flood which will undermine everything that can be removed, it cannot find anything to shake in the wise
builder's hope. He rests on what Christ has done; death
cannot affect that. He believes in a faithful God; and
dying cannot affect that. He believes in the covenant
signed, and sealed, and ratified, in all things ordered well.
He lays hold on the "shalls" and "wills" of an immutable
God, all sealed with the blood of the Redeemer; death
cannot affect any of these. And when the last great trumpet
sounds, and the last fire that shall try every man's work
of what sort it is, comes forth from the throne of God, the
man who in true sincerity and with real experience has laid
hold on Christ, is not afraid of the tremendous hour. What
though the trumpet sounds exceeding loud and long, and

the dead awake, and the angels gather round the great
white throne, and the pillars of heaven tremble, and the
earth is dissolved, and the elements melt with fervent
heat! the man of God feels that the rock on which he
has built can never fail him, and the hope that grace has
given him can never be removed. He smiles serenely amid
it all.

But look at the case of the man whose house is built
on the sand! He could hardly endure the trials of life;
he almost fell under common temptation; he turned his
coat during the hour of persecution; but sorer trials now
await him. Some hypocrites have been bolstered up even
in the last moments, and perhaps have never known that
they were lost till they felt they were; like Dives, of
whom it is written, "In hell he lift up his eyes, being
in torment." He had never lifted up his eyes before; he
did not know his condition till he actually realized it in
all its misery. But the most of men who have come under
the sound of the Gospel, and made a profession, if they
have been deceivers find it out at death, and it must be a
dreadful thing to make that discovery when pain is sharp
and parting is bitter. Ah! dear friend, if you be mistaken
may you find it out now, and not on your dying couch.
May your prayer be, "Lord, show me the worst of my
case. If my profession has been a mistake, O let me not
build up and prop up a rotten thing, but help me to build
aright upon the Rock of Ages." Do pray that prayer, I
beseech you. Remember if death should not teach you the
whole truth of your case, judgment will. There will be
no mistake there, and no opportunity for repentance.
This fallen house was never built again: there was no
salvage from the total wreck. Lost, lost, lost, there is no
word to follow; for once lost, lost for ever! I pray you
if you are a seeker, be not put off with empty hopes and
vain confidences. Buy the truth and sell it not. Lay hold

on eternal life. Seek the true Saviour and be not content till you have Him, for if lost your ruin will be terrible.

Oh, *that lake!* Have you ever read the words, "Shall be cast into the lake of fire, which is the second death"? The lake of fire! and souls cast into it! The imagery is dreadful. "Ah," says one, "that is a metaphor." Yes, I know it is, and a metaphor is but a shadow of the reality. Then, if the shadow be a lake of fire, what must the reality be? If we can hardly bear to think of a "worm that never dieth," and a "fire that never shall be quenched," and of a lake whose seething waves of fire that dash o'er undying and hopeless souls what must hell be in very deed? The descriptions of Scriptures are, after all, but condescensions to our ignorance, partial revealings of fathomless mysteries; but if these are so dreadful, what must the full reality be?

Tempt not your God, neglect not the great salvation, for if you do, you shall not escape. Play not with your souls, be not heedless and careless of the realities of eternity; but now, even now, may God hear your prayer as you breathe it from your inmost souls, and give you truly to be washed in the precious blood, and effectually saved by Him, in whom there is fulness of truth and grace.